MYSTERIUM ARTORIUS

Arthurian Grail Glastonbury Studies

An

Introduction & Evocation

PAUL WESTON

AVALONIAN ÆON
PUBLICATIONS

ISBN: 978-0-9557696-0-3

A CIP catalogue record for this book is
available from the British Library.

Design and text styling by
Bernard Chandler, Glastonbury. www.graffik.co.uk
Cover illustration by Yuri Leitch
Text set in Monotype Bulmer 10/12pt

Printed by HSW Print, Tonypandy, Rhondda, Wales CF40 2XX

ABOUT THE AUTHOR

Paul is a Psychic Questing, Reiki, Crowley, Fellowship of Isis,
Scientology, Adi Da, Kriya Yoga, Mother Meera, Druid, Osho,
Gurdjieff, Anthony Robbins firewalking, Ufological,
Avalon of the Heart, 2012 kind of guy.
www.mysteriumartorius.co.uk

DEDICATION

To Rachel and Michael

ACKNOWLEDGEMENTS

Mother Meera. A living Grail.

John Mappin and *Ted Stourton* at Camelot Castle Hotel Tintagel
for tirelessly championing the importance of creativity.
www.camelotcastle.com

Andrew Collins. For many things but particularly pointing me
in the direction of James Carley's Melkin article and for material on
Joseph of Arimathea that didn't make it into the final version
of *'Twenty-First Century Grail'*.
www.andrewcollins.com

Yuri Leitch. For artwork and providing the stimulus
to finally manifest this work.
www.yurileitch.co.uk

Judith Tripp. For recognising what lies behind this material and
enabling me to road-test it, as it evolved, to successive groups of American
pilgrim tourists in Glastonbury Abbey between 2000 and 2007.

Hank Harrison (who I have never met). For drawing my attention to
Abbot Suger and for his stimulating controversial work on *'Perlesvaus'*.

Geoffrey Ashe. For writing a large number of seriously excellent
books that helped me begin a huge journey.

Chandira Hensey, Fee McBride, and *Chesca Potter* for
Glastonbury Qabalah interaction.

Contents

Preface

THIS WORK HAS ARISEN out of a major writing project called *Avalonian Aeon*, conceived as a Glastonbury autobiography that would include an encyclopaedic introduction to many of its mysteries. It has been my great good fortune to have been involved in some of the psychic questing work of Andrew Collins. He investigated the alleged terrestrial zodiac that surrounds Glastonbury during the eighties and then tested out his findings on a group of people that included myself in 1990. Andy generously made available to me an extraordinary wealth of previously unpublished material to enable me to give a full account of the experience in *Aeon*.

I had deliberately stuffed my head to bursting point with the Arthurian mythos in 1990 in preparation for the Glastonbury Zodiac adventure and this had been crucial in enabling me to experience a major threshold crossing in my life. To do justice to the whole process I decided to lead in to a huge treatment of the Glastonbury Zodiac with an introduction to Arthur and the Grail. It was begun in 2001.

The writing took on a life of its own. I entered into a process that became out of my conscious control. I trawled material from lectures I had originally given to Andy's *Earthquest* group on Arthur and Gurdjieff in 1989. I kept coming back to it. Years went by. The whole of 2004 was permeated by it. I was still adding to it in 2005. As an indicator of the extravagant indulgence of the time, I read John Cowper Powys' thousand page novel *A Glastonbury Romance* three times during a twelve month period. I visited Tintagel and stayed in the wonderful Camelot Castle Hotel on a number of occasions. Some of this book was written in Room 117. There were also trips to Germany where I experienced the awesome blessings of Mother Meera. These journeys usually also involved excursions along the Rhine to the former home of Hildegard of Bingen. This combination of circumstances helped sustain a mood of receptiveness and understanding for the great twelfth century epoch of Grail culture that was supremely satisfying.

The resultant piece was far too long for the main body of the text. It would need massive pruning. I was really happy with what I had written though. I copied it into a new document and saved it with the idea in the back of my mind to maybe one day publish it as a thing in itself. A few other bits of material from elsewhere in *Aeon* could be brought in, some fresh links written, and everything then be blended together.

It has not been my intention to write a comprehensive survey of all aspects of Glastonbury history and mysticism here. Topics omitted are well-covered elsewhere. There are a huge number of books dealing with Arthur, the Grail, Glastonbury, Gothic cathedrals, Knights Templars, Black Madonnas, and so on. People known personally to me such as Andrew Collins, Graham Phillips, and Lynn Picknett and Clive Prince have written extraordinary works on Grail artefacts and the bloodline mysteries spectacularly publicised through *The Da Vinci Code*. I'm always passionately interested in such quests but am concerned that too close a focus on them and their apparent exclusiveness can detract from appreciation of what I would term a culture and a state of consciousness that coheres around the combined elements and is the most inspiring glory of the Middle Ages, something potentially available to all. I have developed an inner sense for what I feel they share in common, call it tongues of fire, the Holy Spirit, Sophianic wisdom, or the Shekinah, all aspects of the spectrum of divine light. On its most simple level, it stimulates creativity and general well-being. This, to me, is Grail conscious-ness. Trying to give the reader a feel for it is my main purpose. As a result therefore, I do not include bloodline considerations or Glastonbury associated artefacts such as the Nanteos cup and the Blue Glass Bowl in my material.

Although there is a tremendous amount of information here, this is a mood piece not a Phd thesis. I have not burdened it with voluminous notes and references. The bibliography should serve to follow up any queries and expand the journey further if so desired. Some of this material may hopefully serve as introductions to other works. If any readers are moved to find *The Krater and the Grail, The Ancient Secret, The Ancient Wisdom*, and *Camelot and the Vision of Albion* as a result of what I have written here I will be most pleased. The sections on *Tintagel of the Heart* and *Glastonbury Qabalah* (a version of which was first published in *Avalon* magazine in summer 1997), although separate in themselves, are important parts of the mood that the preliminary *British Music* seeks to set. Here now is *Mysterium Artorius*.

Paul Weston.
Glastonbury.
September 29th 2007.
Feast of the Archangel Michael.

Introduction

"*Something eternal - universal - the very breath of freedom lives in this land. It stretches out, embracing the whole of humanity. It still speaks to us through the hills and the valleys, the rocks and caves mentioned in the Arthurian legends. The winds and the waves sing of it, the atmosphere is full of it. It is necessary to find contact with this invisible Power which, in only one of its forms, appears as the Arthur of the legend. This Power in reality is the Eternal Spirit of this country —. Could we but realize this, a cultural element would be born again, English in its innermost depths. It speaks to all human beings wherever they live and to whatever nation they belong.*"

Walter Johannes Stein
Is King Arthur a Historical Character?

"*From the perspective of 'science' what matters in a myth is whatever historical elements can be extracted from it. From the perspective that I adopt, what matters in history are all the mythological elements it has to offer.*"

Julius Evola
Revolt Against the Modern World

"*One history passes by in full view, and strictly speaking, is the history of crime, for if there were no crimes there would be no history. All the most important turning-points and stages of this history are marked by crimes: murders, acts of violence, robberies, wars, rebellions, massacres, tortures, executions —
— This is one history, the history which everyone knows, the history which is taught in schools. The other history is the history which is known to very few. For the majority it is not seen at all behind the history of crime. But what is created by this hidden history exists long afterwards, sometimes for many centuries —
The visible history, the history proceeding on the surface, the history of crime, attributes to itself what the hidden history has created. But actually the visible history is always deceived by what the hidden history has created.*"

PD Ouspensky
A New Model of the Universe

I'VE BEEN MOVED and inspired by Arthur and the Grail for a long time. When I was still in infant school, my mother read me bedtime stories by Enid Blyton. This was undoubtedly a formative time of destiny. I could have been introduced to any one of a number of works by the prolific author. I was spared *Don't be Silly Mr Twiddle!*, *The Adventures of Mr Pink Whistle*, and the decidedly dodgy, *The Three Golliwogs*. My mother's choice was *Tales of Brave Adventure*, stories of King Arthur and Robin Hood. From the moment of my first hearing the opening words of the chapter *The Enchanted Sword, "There once lived a King called Uther Pendragon"*, I was hooked. The intensity of my interest ebbed and flowed over the years but always remained.

I had already entered what Jung called *"the primary myth in the collective unconscious of Western Civilisation."* It would lead me to connect with the ideas of fascists and feminists, patriots and pacifists, occultists, mystics, painters, poets, musicians and historians, a whole spectrum of diverse humanity.

It has been my great joy, my ecstasy, to enter into the mystery. I developed methods to enhance my receptivity and pleasure that involved artfully cultivating an ongoing mood, an ambience, a constant background evocation. A relentless combination of history, art, literature, poetry, music, magic, and mysticism, filled me with the spirit of what the great literary seer Peter Ackroyd has called 'English music' which I would adjust to 'British music'. It's like connecting with an indigenous landscape songline. There was nothing parochial and exclusive about the results. My perceptions expanded to welcome in the glories of a supreme epoch of western civilisation, the peak of what I would call Grail culture, centred around the twelfth century, a period with much to teach us in the modern world.

British Music

"Legend and history and the vision of the heart blend
in the building of the Mystical Avalon".

Dion Fortune
Avalon of the Heart

IT BEGINS WITH A SENSE OF PLACE. Arthur's name has been attached
to so many. Glastonbury and Tintagel, best embody the feeling. Regardless
of the strong historical arguments against the validity of their Arthurian associations, something seems to connect the legendary locations that frame his
life from conception to burial. The fundamental factors are landscapes that
profoundly impact on the human psyche, places that will inevitably attract a
numinous mythology.

Neither place is just a repository of history and legend in the past tense,
some kind of museum. That which has given them their unique identity
remains alive and functioning, potent with power for transformation. I would
affirm that there exist certain special places, somehow able to inspire the tribal
tales that any culture needs to understand its identity and needs, its potential
destiny. I believe that Glastonbury and Tintagel seem to be such places,
where history and mythology, two hemispheres of one greater brain, are
almost impossible to separate.

It was surely a mysterious quality of the landscape that attracted people to
Glastonbury in the past. Geoffrey Ashe has noted this in *King Arthur's*
Avalon and *Avalonian Quest*. For example, the Tor can be seen from a considerable distance away. It totally dominates the visual field. As one approaches
and circles around it, a continual shape-shifting is occurring. It presents a
different aspect from every vantage point. And yet, there are places in the
town where the Tor cannot be seen. The view from its summit is extensive
but does not include the abbey, which is hidden by Chalice Hill, apart from
the late addition of the abbot's kitchen. The tower, which is clearly visible
from miles away, doesn't really seem that tall when you're inside it. The early

inhabitants of Britain led lives far more intimately connected to the land than most people do today. The distinctive qualities of the Glastonbury environs would suggest it was a place of the Otherworld. In those far-off times much of the area was underwater as well. The Tor and its adjoining hills would have been virtually islands. Despite subsequent draining much of the spell remains intact. The whole locale seems to participate in an endlessly shifting perspective.

John Cowper Powys in his astounding novel *A Glastonbury Romance* attempted to express, *"the effect of a particular legend, a special myth, a unique tradition, from the remotest past in human history, upon a particular spot on the surface of this planet together with its crowd of inhabitants of every age and of every type of character".* The *'special myth'* is the book's heroine, the Grail, *"much older than Christianity itself"*, for, *"ages before any saint or Saviour of our present Faith appeared in Glastonbury — the earth-goddess had her cauldron of the food of life safely guarded in our Island of the West."* *"Its hero is the Life poured into the Grail. Its message is that no one Receptacle of Life and no one Fountain of Life poured into that Receptacle can contain or explain what the world offers us".*

Powys decided to make the landscape, history, and mythology of Glastonbury a character in his novel. The different elements cannot be separated. They constitute an elusive *something* that can interact with a person as strongly as a human character, stirring passion, idealism, madness, asceticism, horror, mysticism, and eroticism in all possible combinations. This approach would later be developed in the psychogeographical London work of Peter Ackroyd and Iain Sinclair.

During the nineteen-twenties HV Morton had visited Glastonbury as part of a nationwide car journey that resulted in the hugely successful book, *In Search of England.* He had noted that *"It is, perhaps, not strange that all places which have meant much to Man are filled with an uncanny atmosphere, as if something were still happening there secretly: as if filled with a hidden life. Glastonbury is like that."*

The occultist Dion Fortune may well have been familiar with the work. In her mystical, poetic book about Glastonbury, *Avalon of the Heart,* she wrote that, *"Where strong spiritual emotions have been felt for long periods of time by successive generations of dedicated men or women - especially if they have had among them those who may be reckoned as saints because of their genius for devotion - the mental atmosphere of the place becomes imbued with spiritual forces, and sensitive souls capable of response are deeply stirred thereby when they come to it".*

Fortune wondered if we *"miss much when we abandon the ancient custom of pilgrimage?"* *"Every race has its holy centres, places where the veil is thin",* that contain, *"power to quicken the spiritual life and vitalise the soul with fresh enthusiasm and inspiration."* *"Glastonbury is a spiritual volcano wherein the fire that is at the heart of the British race breaks through and flames to heaven".*

Tintagel is another such place. Many would agree that the area around the cliff-top castle ruins by the sea carries an archaic feeling of tangible magic. Imagine the end of a perfect summer day. The all but cloudless sky has become a symphony of gradations of portentous pink focused on the sun setting into the sea. As its reflection touches the water, a rippling ray spreads out from the horizon back across the foaming Mediterranean turquoise waves to the beach, like a sword of shimmering light. From a vantage point up on the cliffs, amongst a riot of small wild flowers, looking across at the ruined castle and down to the entrance of the famous Merlin's Cave, one can forget all the intellectual arguments of history, feel the Arthurian mythos alive in the very air, and *believe.* Wordsworth's famous lines on the landscape around Tintern Abbey come readily to mind.

> *"And I have felt*
> *A presence that disturbs me with the joy*
> *Of elevated thoughts; a sense sublime*
> *Of something far more deeply interfused*
> *Whose dwelling is the light of setting suns,*
> *And the round ocean and the living air,*
> *And the blue sky, and in the mind of man:*
> *A motion and a spirit, that impels*
> *All thinking things, all objects of thought,*
> *And rolls through all things."*

Place stirs feeling. Inspires poetic mystical sensibilities. Fills the heart with the intuition of music that is constantly present if not always audible. During the late nineteenth and early twentieth century there was a great British musical revival that produced a huge corpus of work inspired by love of the landscape. Perhaps the most famous examples are *The Lark Ascending* and *Fantasia on a Theme by Thomas Tallis* by Ralph Vaughan Williams. Both pieces were composed just before the First World War. In retrospect, they do seem to carry an incredible nostalgia for a vanished world and lost generation, but they also speak of some more archaic mystical quality of supreme sublime beauty that remains an ever-present force emanating from the very earth of our sacred *'sceptred isle'.* Williams' third symphony and the haunting first movement of the fifth can produce a similar response. The obvious superstar of the scene was Elgar. He is primarily known for his Last Night of the Proms anthem, *Pomp and Circumstance,* which includes the great soundtrack of Edwardian imperialism, *Land of Hope and Glory.* I feel that's rather unfortunate as it gives a very one-dimensional sense of the man and has possibly kept some people from wanting to investigate him further. Elgar composed many works inspired by nature and the nostalgia of childhood that are in turn, passionate, wistful, melancholic, mellow, and mystical.

As a small child he would sit by the banks of the River Severn, *"trying to write down what the reeds were saying".* This continued into his adult life as he walked and bicycled around the Malvern Hills. In a letter to a friend he said, *"the trees are singing my music or have I sung theirs?"* There's a visionary sequence in Ken Russell's inspired 1962 black and white BBC drama documentary on Elgar which depicts him as a young man riding on a white horse across the Malverns to the stirring accompaniment of the *Introduction and Allegro for Strings* and shafts of sunlight.

A number of the more prominent composers of the great revival were mystically inclined with interests in Celtic and Arthurian mythology, faery lore, and so on. They were not of the status of Beethoven and Wagner but are unfairly neglected. Bax, Bantock, Butterworth, Delius, Finzi, and Ireland, all help to back up Vaughan Williams and Elgar very nicely in creating an evocational soundscape.

Ralph Vaughan Williams and John Cowper Powys were both born in 1872 and lived to truly ripe old age, producing stunning work well into their seventies. As people they were considerably different. In his *Autobiography,* Powys gives little space to music. To me though, both men expressed something poignant and powerful that was quintessentially of the land and its history.

A Glastonbury Romance and the music of Vaughan Williams became inseparable in my consciousness. Powys had said that, *"the symbolism of the Grail represents a lapping up of one perfect drop of noon-day happiness as Nietzsche in his poignant words would say, or as Nature herself, according to the hint given us by Goethe, whispers to us in more voices than at present we are able to hear, or to understand when we do hear."* A particular Avalon of the Heart reverie of mine became my personal expression of that idea: a May morning on the Tor, the unique Somerset mystical misty blueness of the sky around the horizon's rim providing a perfect backdrop for ascending larksong. Blossom and blooming abound as the landscape rolls away like surging strings, a hymn of ancestral voices, ever young and hopeful.

In John Michell's *City of Revelation* I first read of the idea of

Glastonbury's Perpetual Choir. Apparently, a Dark Age work known as the Welsh Triads mentioned three "perpetual choirs of Britain". These were ecclesiastical establishments where relay teams of monks kept up a constant liturgical chant. They were located at Amesbury, just down the road from Stonehenge, Llantwit Major in South Wales, and Glastonbury. Michell noted some kind of alignment relationship between the sites and extrapolated geometrical data that led him to talk of a "Circle of Perpetual Choirs". Elgar's Malverns were in the centre of it. The material seemed a bit vague but something about this idea inspired me in a way I couldn't yet make fully conscious.

Rudyard Kipling's classic children's tale, *Puck of Pook's Hill* provides another potential doorway into the zone. The story begins with two children in a fairy ring in woods near their home. They give a little performance of selected extracts from *Midsummer Night's Dream* on the eve of the very night itself. This conjures up Puck, the ancient spirit of the hills. *"I came into England with Oak, Ash and Thorn, and when Oak, Ash and Thorn are gone I shall go too."* He has watched all of history pass by with a benevolent and mischievous eye, occasionally intervening in human affairs.

Puck becomes the children's guide for a history lesson of their immediate locale. From this particular saga, involving landmarks familiar to them, the greater vista of the life of the whole British nation unfolds. They meet a Roman soldier who goes off to serve on Hadrian's Wall, a Saxon from the time of the Norman conquest, a Jew from the Magna Carta epoch, and so on. With Puck we encounter not only humans but old gods as well. The cult of Mithras is sympathetically portrayed. The narrative continuity comes through a rune covered singing sword made by Saxon deity turned smith, Weland. The sword has a subtle auspicious effect on the lives of the subsequent generations, leading through to Magna Carta. Through all this Kipling affirms the diverse elements in the layers of history that make the mixture that is Britain.

The idea of Puck watching from ancient hills enhanced my sense of 'British music'. The feeling of a primordial past somehow still living through the very land itself and the ongoing mythos it generates became ever stronger for me. The land has a consciousness of some kind. A voice that can be heard. A feeling that can be communicated. At certain places and times, on hills at dawn and sunset, by wells, streams and rivers, in moonlit woods, amongst poignant ruins and remains, it lingers on, surprisingly potent, waiting to inspire in diverse circumstances; poets, soldiers, musicians, mystics, militants, all ages and genders across the whole social spectrum.

Such is the preparatory ambience. A number of powerful ideas are coming together. At least in some poetic sense, Glastonbury, the Avalon of the Heart, is a perpetual choir that is helping to compose and to play 'British music', an expression of some vast mystical landscape mystery. All of our great artists, from the designers of Stonehenge and Glastonbury Abbey through to Powys and Vaughan Williams are part of Albion's greater perpetual choir. Its supreme symphony, in which untold multitudes have participated in innumerable ways in every epoch from the megalithic to the present is the mythos of Arthur and the Grail.

Arthur

ARCHAIC DEITY

M Y ADULT ENTHUSIASM for Arthur was undoubtedly catalysed by the
magnificent 1981 movie, *Excalibur*. Repeated viewings of it had
increasingly stimulated my archetypal imagination. Its richly realised scenes
were like living oil paintings, passionately enlivened by the rousing music of
Wagner and Orff. A mythologically literate script linked the vivid tableaux
together. The background to the film was an interesting one. Director John
Boorman had read *A Glastonbury Romance* in the fifties and was inspired by
the desire to make some kind of movie based upon it. He had come to
Glastonbury and sat on the top of the Tor as far back as 1961, full of this idea.
He kept the hope alive throughout the time that he made his name in the
movie business with such masterpieces as *Deliverance*. Eventually it became
clear that it simply wasn't going to happen. The impetus was channelled into
Excalibur, where the quirky depiction of Merlin was influenced by Powys'
portrayal in his last great novel, *Porius*.

It was Geoffrey Ashe's *Camelot and the Vision of Albion* that became my
most useful doorway into the Arthurian enigma. The work arose from Ashe's
involvement in an archaeological dig at Cadbury Castle. Situated near to
the Somerset-Dorset border, Cadbury is a hill-fort primarily of the same
immediately pre-Roman epoch as Maiden Castle. It participates in the shape-
shifting magic of the greater Glastonbury landscape in as much as the Tor is
visible enough from its summit but the line of sight doesn't work both ways.

Cadbury's fame derives from its Arthurian associations. At the time of
Henry VIII, the antiquarian John Leland went walkabout around the landscape, recording items of interest. *"At South Cadbyri standith Camallate,
sumtyme a famose toun or castelle. The people can tell nothing thar but that
they have hard say that Arture much resortid to Camalat."* This is the first
written link of the place with Arthur's famous base. It's not much to go on.
'Traditional tales' of the locals can't be accurately traced before Leland.
Nonetheless, an ambience hung about the place and its associations that nagged
at the back of diverse minds across the centuries until the genius loci conspired
to create the appropriate moment to begin the modern Arthurian revival.

Major archaeological work occurred at Cadbury during mythological 1967, when so many strange things were stirring. The dig was highly publicised, being featured in the press and the medium of the moment, television. At the peak of the Summer of Love, the Beatles had broadcast *All you Need is Love* to an unprecedented global TV audience. The events at Cadbury may not have reached the same numbers but something significant was seen to be in motion. The hilltop occupies a large area. It was possible to allow the general public to visit without disrupting the work. An unexpectedly high number did so. The charisma of Arthur clearly lived on, and in ways that the organisers of the dig had not anticipated.

The Camelot of the romances and Hollywood movies was a medieval construct. There was no way that anything remotely resembling it was going to be uncovered. This didn't seem to deter people at all. It wasn't as if the visitors were purely and simply hung-up on nebulous mythology. What did the dig discover? During the period of the major Saxon incursions after the departure of the legions, Cadbury was refortified on a scale all but unknown elsewhere in the country. Whoever was responsible was obviously a figure of power and prestige, an 'Arthur type'. No inscriptions bearing his name came to light. Many still doubt the associations of Arthur with the South West. Advocates of Scotland and North Wales make powerful cases. Nonetheless, the whole business was more than enough to help recast a new form of the spell. Since the Cadbury dig the level of interest and ever-increasing knowledge and understanding of the period once generally known as the Dark Ages has gone through a spectacular exponential increase. Alongside this, the romance of the Arthurian mythos has in no way diminished. On the contrary, it has been astonishingly revitalised.

Mystics who talk about the 'spirit of history' and the 'world-historical-process' sometimes point to the apt timing of particular archaeological discoveries. The Dead Sea Scrolls, for example, were recovered just after the apocalyptic world war, just before the re-founding of the state of Israel, nicely in time for a bit of theological controversy to lead into the millennial end-time. The earliest days of the Christian era stirred up again. Might there be something significant about the timing of the Summer of Love Cadbury dig? Arthur seemed to be announcing that he and everything he represented was going to be an integral part of the consciousness revolution, at least as far as the British side of it was concerned.

Geoffrey Ashe served as secretary for the dig. He was moved to ponder just where the enthusiasm for the project came from and what it meant. What is the mystique, the charisma of Arthur, and what kind of response has it brought forth from people through the ages and into the present day?

He found answers by paying close attention to a seemingly obscure statement by Britain's greatest visionary poet, William Blake. *"The giant Albion, was Patriarch of the Atlantic; he is the Atlas of the Greeks, one of those the Greeks called Titans. The stories of Arthur are the acts of Albion, applied to a Prince of the fifth century."*

Firstly, Albion seems to be an ancient name for Britain. The Titans were the original Greek gods before the famous Olympian pantheon. They represented a culture supplanted by later migrations of other peoples, events mythologised as their defeat and banishment by the new wave of Zeus and co. Dim memories of their epoch persisted, taking on the glow of a golden age. It came to be associated with Cronus or Saturn. His consort was Rhea, worshipped particularly in Crete as the Great Mother. The Greek Hesiod described the Saturnian age as a paradisiacal time when humanity was sustained by the fruits of the land, and nobody ever grew old. The nostalgia of its allure has inspired visionaries as diverse as John Cowper Powys and John Michell. The depth of response to the quest for the recovery of Britain's lost prehistory may owe something to it.

Through their migrations the megalithic peoples link Britain with the Mediterranean and also to the cult of the mother goddess and the dead. Britain's 'prehistoric' era, of West Kennet long barrow, Silbury Hill, Avebury and Stonehenge, seems to hang together in the dreamtime of Albion as a unity, although it extended over millennia that saw waves of successive cultural changes resulting from incoming migrants and developing technologies from stone through bronze to iron. At first the underworld was open to all, the home of beloved ancestors and the mother goddess. Sites such as West Kennet weren't just tombs but communal centres where seasonal gatherings would probably have been celebrated. Women may have come to give birth in them. Some kind of hallucinogenic beverage might have been shared giving ecstatic dissolution in the collective dreamtime and connection to oracular sources of wisdom.

Golden Age beliefs about the underworld and a mother goddess were rejected by the solar warrior culture of the Bronze Age. West Kennet long barrow was sealed up with tons of debris. This was one form that the British version of the banishment of Cronos took. Some have argued that the Bronze Age culture of the Wessex chieftains of Stonehenge provided formative strata in the Arthurian mythos, not unlike the Homeric heroic literature of the same era.

The Celtic period saw a return of respect for the female and the collective dead. Nostalgia for the past is not a recent British cultural trait caused by loss of empire and an uncertain future. It has manifested throughout our history. The great megalithic sites would have stimulated awe and mythology to later

generations hundreds and even thousands of years after they were constructed. British Celtic culture seems to reflect that. It would also be a mistake to
think that the Neolithic peoples had simply been wiped out or disappeared.
They were still around and something of their beliefs would have inevitably
persisted. A blend was forming.

The Greek Cronus was banished to an island realm in the west. Later
sources speak of a British Cronos, imprisoned in a cave on some far western
island, resting in eternal sleep from which he uttered strange prophecies.
These details don't fit the Greek myth and therefore may apply to an indigenous deity in some way analogous to Cronos. Robert Graves and Geoffrey
Ashe identified the Celtic Bran as a possible contender. Medieval Welsh
legends, clearly full of archaic material, mention him as a giant monarch. The
name of Bran means 'raven' which in Greek is *corone*, close enough to
Cronos, and a raven was associated with the Titan.

Bran the Blessed ruled in London. His severed head became a potent
magical object. Buried at Tower Hill, it protected the realm and spoke
prophecies. An Irish form of Bran went on a sea voyage to otherwordly
islands where time stood still. He also waded out across the Irish Sea. Blake
has a passage where his Albion falls into a prolonged deathly sleep in a
manner that seems a clear pointer to the British Cronos. A reawakening is
being invoked, and with it, the return of the golden age. Geoffrey Ashe realised
that with Cronos-Albion-Bran we have a, *"'Patriarch of the Atlantic' spanning
the Ocean and its islands; asleep or in abeyance now, withdrawn to a cave in
a blissful western isle of his own, yet not dead or finally irrelevant. Obviously
the Arthur of Avalonian legend is beginning to glimmer on the horizon."*

Celtic culture was never totally suppressed by the Romans. Centuries
later, as the empire declined, temple shrines began to appear on the old
prominences again. There is evidence for such at Cadbury, Maiden and
Brean Down. The most notable was at Lydney in Gloucestershire, a dream
incubation temple to Nodens whose son was Gwyn ap Nudd, famously
linked to Glastonbury Tor.

The spirit of Albion stirred again, and as the Romans departed, found
expression in the form of Arthur. The multiple British locations we now find
bearing his name are, *"the bones of Albion reanimated by Arthur"*. Geoffrey
Ashe summarised the continuity. *"Like Bran 'the Blessed', Arthur embodies
the glory of the island of Britain, and presides over a noble era which he is, so
to speak, the spirit of. Like Bran, he leads British forces overseas; and his
Annwn quest has likenesses to Bran's invasion of Ireland which are beyond
coincidence. Like Bran, he is mortally wounded yet still mysteriously alive.
Bran, through the burial of his head on Tower Hill, goes on protecting Britain;*

and a triad tells how Arthur explicitly took over this function from him by digging the head up, saying Britain should rely on valour alone. — Bran is the raven; and according to a folklore belief, the ever-living Arthur revisits Britain in that guise."

Probably the strongest association of Arthur with archaic religious consciousness comes in his link with the Wild Hunt. This mind-bending phenomenon has been recorded all over northern Europe and is often associated with Norse beliefs. The basic idea is of a group of ghostly riders who appear on particular nights, often accompanied by archetypal hell-hounds, chilling horn blasts, and demonic hubbub. They may be led by some notable figure, perhaps a deity or historical hero, who will vary with the location. The recently dead might be scooped up to accompany them to the underworld. For much of their journey they fly through the sky but will periodically touch down to follow stretches of haunted paths and roadways.

The study of the roots and development of the Wild Hunt is a vast and engrossing one. There are numerous records of practices that seem to be rooted in archaic shamanism involving the ingestion of hallucinogens to induce an out of the body experience that enables someone to somehow join the airborne group. There are problems in determining quite what kind of reality is involved because the Hunt has often been witnessed by frightened sober bystanders as a seemingly physical phenomenon. Incredibly enough there are twentieth century accounts of its appearance.

Arthur became known as a leader of the Wild Hunt across Europe before the written romances appeared. He is depicted on a mosaic floor dating from about 1163 at Otranto cathedral in Italy riding on a goat. We can assume the motif was already well established. He also is spoken of in a twelfth century Sicilian source as living inside the volcanic Mount Etna, thus showing how his name had become associated with another widespread folk archetype of the time, the hero in the hollow hill.

The Wild Hunt is said to ride out from Cadbury Castle in the direction of Glastonbury. There are variations on the details and timing of the event but Midsummer Eve seems to be a favourite. The king and his knights follow a path that has come to be known as Arthur's Hunting Causeway. Geoffrey Ashe's time spent at Cadbury helped inspire him to produce a magnificent depiction of the Wild Hunt in its full disturbing glory as part of a visionary episode in his 1973 novel *The Finger and the Moon,* which brings together Arthur and Gwyn ap Nudd, White Son of Night.

It all begins with a repeated *"strident terrible horn blast"* that shook the whole of Cadbury Castle as the landscape all around starts to strangely glow. *"The Great Bear wavered in the sky and its shape altered. Polaris lurched sideways. New lights glared over the Mendips like supernovae.*" Far away in the vicinity of the Tor, a white shadow appears and enlarges as if moving nearer. *"Different noises were mingling now, a medley of unhuman bayings, and the white form was convoyed by smaller ones that had firefly-sparks of red dancing above them.*" On the Cadbury ramparts a group of about fifty horsemen had assembled and begun slowly moving forward to the old gateway. *"They were hideous. These were dressed up corpses rather than men. Skulls with decaying flesh and thin strands of beard sat on bodies upheld by stiff leather as much as by their own firmness".* *"The men rode without stirrups. They wore metal-studded leather jerkins and breeches, and cloaks pinned to their right shoulders. Spears, long swords, and white cross-marked shields were slung around them. Most of them were stocky and bare-headed, but a helmeted group at the front included one who was tall."* The Arthur figure's helmet hid his face and had a scarlet dragon on its crest.

"The white Tor wraiths had reached the hill and were floating above the old gateway. The largest had condensed into a nebulously human figure, also on horseback." The two groups faced each other. Arthur's knights likewise became airborne. He, *"joined the White One, drawing so close alongside that they almost merged"* and now brandished a horn whose next blast set the whole group off across the sky together towards the Tor. *"Hooves brushed the tree-tops and made them tingle with fire."*

"A comet-tail of newcomers kept forming behind. More and more ex-humans gathered and were launched into space. Few of these were mounted. Most went on foot, those that still had feet. Many moved as if they were being dragged. Men, women, children, and lumps of flesh which I believe were stillbirths and abortions, swarmed in zero-gravity over the hilltop and soared off in the wake of the first company, drawn by a suction that did not disturb the air. Half of them perhaps had tatters of clothing. The styles of the garments on those collapsing frames seemed to span many centuries. Roman style armour, Elizabethan ruffs, even Victorian top-hats and boys' sailor suits, made parts of the mob into nauseous masquerades. They swept in to rendezvous on the hill from vast perspectiveless spaces, generation upon generation of vanished sons and daughters of Albion, they converged along pathways of pale fire – laser-beams traversing the map – and fell in behind those who were already depart-ing. All with an incessant murmur that swelled to a hubbub without ever becoming speech."

Thirty years after the famous dig, in 1998, Cadbury gave up its most suggestive secret yet. It was a Bronze Age era burial. A male in a coffin, over eight feet in length, made of pieces of wood bound at the ends to look like a boat. He was laid out in such a manner as to be clearly pointing towards the distant Tor. It wouldn't be too controversial an inference to suggest that the hill was seen as an Annwn/Avalon-type isle of the dead. There's an obvious similarity to Arthur's famous last journey. The medieval material really does contain millennia old motifs that were present long before the Dark Age warlord. Arthur as echo of some primal deity may not be as far-fetched an idea as it has occasionally seemed. To think of Arthur as Lord of the Dead can be a very potent idea. In this role he is ruler of the ancestors, all of them, from the Stone Age to the Somme and beyond.

'DARK AGE' HISTORY

It is certainly useful, alongside attempts to get a feeling for the archaic mythic Arthur, to try and understand something of the bigger picture of the period in which Arthur and Merlin, if they were in any way historical characters, were believed to have lived. The departure of the Roman legions in 410 AD doesn't now appear to have been quite the disaster it was once considered to be. The old infrastructure began to break down and towns shrank in size with buildings falling into decay. There was a reversion to pre-Roman tribalism. Despite all of this, there are many indications of cultural strength and vitality. A number of large new structures arose around the realm amidst the increasingly neglected ruins. Contact with the external world did not exactly cease. Considerable trade was maintained. A distinctive Christianity flourished. There were incursions from assorted peoples who could be characterised as invaders or migrants. This was a cause of increasing instability. Nonetheless, fifty years or so after the Roman departure, the old province of Britannia was in good shape.

Although Rome had been sacked by the Visigoths in 410, that event didn't bring about the immediate end of the empire. It lingered on, although in a considerably weakened form. Belief in its revival had not entirely faded. A British contingent actually travelled to France in 470 to fight for the Emperor Anthemius. From this it's clear that the feeling of being part of the Roman world remained strong. Within six years however, the last western emperor was deposed. This event marked the end of only one half of the empire.

Constantine had created a new capital for the Roman Empire at the city he massively rebuilt in his own name. The empire divided into a western and eastern part. It was the western side, based in Rome, which had crumbled under barbarian assault. The eastern Byzantine Empire survived with its own emperor. The most famous of all its rulers was Justinian. In the early part of the sixth century he set about trying to re-conquer the lost western realms.

His endeavours were spectacularly successful. North Africa was reclaimed. Italy itself was regained. There were extensive trading connections between the western British kingdom of Dumnonia, which included Somerset and Cornwall, and the Byzantine Empire. These increased in intensity during Justinian's time. This would have helped to give credibility to any pro-Roman factions. If the barbarian tribes could be defeated elsewhere, then why not in Britain?

The timescale generally suggested for Arthur's campaigns is very close to the triumphs of Justinian, who reigned from 527 to 565. One of the fragments we have concerning Arthur's battles mentions how he displayed an iconic image of the Virgin Mary on his shield and, thus protected, single handed massacred his opponents. This kind of prowess reached its gory climax at his most famous victory, Badon, where the mighty warlord was solely responsible for slaughter on a huge scale. Some have doubted this Marian devotion but her cult was powerful in the Byzantine Empire where both armies and navies went into battle displaying her image. Arthur is being portrayed as a Christian here. Was this just the propaganda of revisionist scribes centuries later? Why the Virgin Mary?

The Arthurian period was one of immense dramatic traumatic change. Numerous sources mention various details which when put together show that, for approximately twenty years in the middle of the sixth century, Britain experienced a truly remarkable sequence of natural phenomenon that ultimately had world shaping significance. The situation resembled something from the pages of *Revelation*. Those who lived though it could be forgiven for thinking that the End Times were upon them.

Whenever apocalyptic scenarios are discussed, one of the most obvious scene-setters will be signs in the sky of some kind. In the first major written source for the story of Arthur, Geoffrey of Monmouth's *History of the Kings of Britain*, prophecies of Merlin introduce the life of Arthur in an epoch of danger and despair *"when the very sky was falling down and when the wrath of the stars dried up the crops in the very fields."* Most dramatic of all is the appearance of *"a star of great magnitude and brilliance, with a single beam shining from it. At the end of this beam was a ball of fire, spread out in the shape of a dragon. From the dragon's mouth stretched forth two rays of light — the second split up into seven smaller shafts of light. The star appeared three times, and all who saw it were struck with fear and wonder."* The event immediately precedes the coming to power of Uther, who derives his 'dragon head' designation from the portent following Merlin's assurance of its auspiciousness for him and the destiny of a future son he will sire.

In 524 there were two long periods, punctuated by the sight of a comet visible for twenty days, where the stars 'ran' from evening to daybreak. Halley's comet made a spectacular appearance in 530 and was duly recorded. 531 and 532 saw episodes of exceptional meteor showers. In 533 and 535 there were notable comets and then in 538 Zacharias of Mithylene chronicled that a *"great and terrible comet appeared in the sky at evening time for one hundred days."*

Dendrochronological tree-ring evidence shows strong indications of extreme climatic disruption in Britain then. Investigation of the ice core of Greenland likewise reveals the presence of a major dust veil filled with sulphur, seemingly caused by volcanic eruption or cometary impact, possibly in water, perhaps also with atmospheric detonations. This affected a huge area including the Americas, Britain, and the Mediterranean. 536 saw the densest longest case of dry fog in historical records. Byzantine historian Procopius wrote that *"the sun gave forth its light without brightness like the moon"* for a whole year. Michael the Syrian recorded that *"Each day it shone for about four hours, and still this light was only a feeble shadow"*. It was the second coldest summer in 1500 years. A number of entire years around that time were similarly amongst the very coldest in a millennium. In such grim conditions fruit didn't ripen properly. There was famine in Ireland during the 530s and 40's. This period helped establish pre-conditions for a ghastly culmination.

Comets have long been seen as portents. The general feeling associated with them has often been trepidation in anticipation of potential disaster and upheaval. The long period of intense aerial omens concluded in 542 when an outbreak of bubonic plague began in the Middle East. The Black Death of 1348 is well known. A third of Europe's population perished. Strangely neglected in the general sense of European history is the Justinian plague. The whole Mediterranean world was trashed by it. Byzantine expansion halted. In fact, the empire never recovered. It was permanently weakened and unable to fully resist the emergence of Mohammed's Islam barely a century later.

The pestilence reached Britain in 549 through the Byzantine trading routes. Decades of climatic degeneration had already created a wasteland. The Romano British kingdoms were devastated by the plague. It has been speculated that the population was reduced by 60 percent. A number of locations seem to have been completely abandoned.

Visitors to Tintagel may sometimes feel a poignant melancholy, reminiscent of the Glastonbury Abbey mood, where a sense of tragic loss is often discernable. There is good reason for this. It seems likely that the great plague may have entered the country at Tintagel. Archaeology has established that during the Dumnonia post-Roman Arthurian era it was a high prestige site, probably royally connected, that was the centre of trade with the Byzantine Empire. From golden citadel to centre of death in a virtual instant would have registered in the locale as a huge inexplicable trauma. The place seems to have ceased to function for centuries.

There were further minor outbreaks of plague throughout Europe during the rest of the century. Climatic abnormalities continued after the great plague, a severe winter in 545 and 554, a storm in London in 548 so intense that 250 people were killed, five months of violent rain in Scotland in 552, exceptional thunderstorms all over Britain in 555, and so on.

Revelation provided a kind of checklist to measure events against to see if the last days were at hand. The Wormwood star falls from heaven causing widespread death. A great multiple headed dragon appears in the heavens. Its tail brings down the stars. In 431 the Council of Ephesus proclaimed Mary as Theotokos, the Mother of God. She became more clearly identified with the *"great portent"* of the *"woman clothed with the sun, with the moon under her feet"* who was confronted by the dragon. It was war in heaven. Archangel Michael fought the dragon and his angels. The most notable visionary manifestation of the great sword bearer, featuring strong hints of celestial phenomenon, occurred at Mount Garganus in Italy. One source gives 536 as the date, right in the middle of the dust veil upheaval. And Babylon in the form of Rome was finally falling.

Seeing the Arthurian period against this backdrop: dragon comets and plague, famine and Marian icons, recalling an idea of Rudolf Steiner that Arthur was under the command of Archangel Michael, we can begin to understand why it generated a potent enduring mythology. All this arises out of very real events. In Britannia hope had arisen. Rome seemed to revive through the Byzantines. The moment of destiny called forth a triumphant hero. Everywhere the enemy was routed. But crops were failing. A bleak permanent winter descended. Pestilence ravaged the land. When it was all over, the age of Arthur was gone. The details of his passing were unknown. The Saxons had not suffered as badly from the plague. They were left in the ascendant. Britain's history had been changed forever. The emotions generated by such events would surely be sufficient to inspire tales that would be told around the fires for centuries. The theme of the wasteland, the idea of the loss of the Grail and the figure of the Fisher King could well owe much of their later form to memories of those terrifying times.

The first reference to Arthur is found in a text dating from about three hundred years after his alleged life. *The History of the Britons* by Nennius seems to have been composed in the early ninth century. The hero is mentioned as fighting against Saxon invaders. Twelve battles are listed. The last of these, Badon, was a major victory that ensured peace for a generation. The tenth century *Annals of Wales,* generally accepted as containing far older material, likewise mentions Arthur and Badon, giving it a date of 516 AD. An immediate problem arises from the fact that a major source for the Badon epoch, Gildas' *On the Ruin of Britain,* written barely fifty years afterwards, mentions the battle but not Arthur. It would probably be possible to fill a vast library with the literature expended on all matters arising from this scant material.

People may still be arguing about Arthur as a possible megalithic era or Iron Age deity and his historicity in another hundred years from now. What does seem fairly clear is that, whatever the case, between the period of the apparently historical Arthur's life and his later career as European superstar, he became a kind of Celtic messiah. Hermann of Laon wrote of an instructive episode that had occurred in Devon in 1113 during a visit by a group of French monks. A heated dispute arose when they were scornful of the local belief that Arthur was somehow still alive. The doubters were lucky to escape unharmed. The hopes of the peoples who had been pushed ever further westwards by the Saxon incursions were passionately focused on the once and future king. The Welsh *Black Book of Carmarthen,* which was compiled about 1200 but contains material generally acknowledged as much older, summarises this sentiment, in verses known as *The Stanzas of the Graves,* with the famous words that Powys used to begin *A Glastonbury Romance,* *"Not wise (the thought) a grave for Arthur."*

In that *Black Book* Arthur features in distinctly otherworld adventures. The stories told of him are full of Celtic religious mythology. His comrades include Mabon son of Modron and Manawydan son of Llyr. These were Celtic Gods. They fight with dog-headed beings. *The Spoils of Annwn* is another Welsh work that, although also only written down about 1200, has been considered to be full of authentic archaic Celtic motifs. It does seem to be an early form of the Grail quest. Arthur and his men sail in a ship to the otherworld island of Annwn in order to seize a magic cauldron. None but the brave could eat from it. It is kindled by the breath of nine maidens. Annwn also gets referred to as the fortress of glass. Timespace is generally wonky there. It's dark at noon. Hardly anyone returns from the exploit.

Such was the long alchemical incubation of the Celtic elements of the Arthurian mythos as the Anglo Saxon peoples consolidated their gains until the mysterious entity we call England began to emerge and, on another twist of the historical spiral, a hero such as Alfred the Great could be thought of as its defender and just law giver.

THE NORMAN MATRIX

Our perceptions of historical events are continually recast by the cumulative experiences of each passing century. The Norman conquest of 1066 perhaps seems more vivid when we look at it through the filter of recent times. Nazi style and efficiency was introduced to the new domain. The Anglo Saxons were ethnically cleansed as a totalitarian racist elite imposed slavery and degradation upon them. Any rebellion was met with a response reminiscent of the eastern front in 1941.Women and children were routinely massacred. Villages were incinerated, land laid waste. Survivors endured a diet of grass and rats. A huge number of castles were built across the country to maintain control. Churches were torn down and replaced by new buildings in grander Norman style. The old ruling class was virtually exterminated. In the first century after the conquest there was scarcely any intermarriage between the Normans and English. The percentage stayed low amongst the highest level of aristocracy for a further century. French and Latin were the languages of culture, government, and control. English was the tongue of peasant untermensch, worthy only of contempt. It was about three hundred years before it really reasserted itself. Whether the conquest was ultimately good for the nation's karma or not still gets argued about in the present day. The short-term effect was widespread lamentation, wailing, and gnashing of teeth.

The Normans put themselves about a bit. The conquest of England was not their only adventure. Sicily had come under Muslim control in the ninth century. All kinds of esoteric stuff jostled with Greek learning and proto-science in a potent pressure-cooker. Enter the Normans. They'd begun manoeuvring themselves into southern Italy during the early eleventh century. Eventually they tried to conquer Sicily. The pope even pronounced it a crusade. A sequence of efforts was partially successful. The enterprise was put on-hold when a number of those involved joined William on his trip to Hastings.

By 1091, Sicily was a Norman kingdom. It wasn't occupied with the same thoroughness as England. Numbers involved were far smaller. At the same time that the Normans were consolidating the assimilation of England, they were encountering the extraordinary culture of Sicily. It's an eye-opener to contemplate them there, living like Arab caliphs, with exotic palaces and gardens, harems, and eunuchs. Entertainment wouldn't necessarily be roast oxen and a piss-up whilst giving the locals a kicking and raping the women. Poetry recitals, dancing girls, music. Scholars from the three desert-monotheisms worked together. Learning thrived. They remained in control there for a century. The Normans in Sicily were in many ways a group unto themselves who were not politically connected with those in Britain. Nonetheless, there were links. All kinds of influences could have subtly found their way into England.

William the Conqueror had created a cross-channel empire. It briefly divided between his sons but soon reunited with the advent of Henry I. The governing elite of the newly forming kingdom sought to establish an identity and credibility for it to set alongside some of its illustrious European neighbours. They were also curious about the Celts, who they were encountering along the borders of their new kingdom, as they were old adversaries of the Saxons, telling tales of a great hero who had successfully defeated them. It was against this background that Geoffrey of Monmouth's *History of the Kings of Britain,* appeared in 1135.

Geoffrey may have been Welsh or Breton. He came to live in Oxford, possibly working as a teacher. His work was presented as factual and based on information contained in an ancient document he had obtained from his uncle. Anyone wishing to investigate it will face immediate problems. The name of almost every person featured, every location named, has been disputed in rival theories. The study of his potential sources is ongoing. During the Middle Ages his tales were regarded as historical truth. Later generations came to consider Geoffrey as purely a writer of fiction. Tentative rehabilitation of his reputation progressed during the twentieth century.

Maybe some of his stories do contain genuinely archaic strata. The references to a comet and pestilence may well be part of an authentic tradition he had access to. Geoffrey gives the first written account we have that names Tintagel as the place of Arthur's conception. Why would he have done that? Modern archaeology has shown that the now ruinous castle was not constructed until after Geoffrey's work. It may well be that it was intended to gain prestige through association and also to clearly show Norman control of an earlier power site. The place had been comparatively deserted since the time of the plague. Oral tradition of some kind may have preserved the memory of Tintagel's prestige during the time of Arthur.

The work was an immediate major success. It wove a kind of foundation myth for the emerging Norman British consciousness, giving a classical pedigree to the monarchy. The Romans liked to believe that they were descended from Aeneas, a refugee from the Trojan war. Geoffrey tells the tale of his great-grandson, Brutus, who found his way with a boatload of companions to the ancient isle of Albion. The Trojan contingent landed at Totnes and battled some giants before going on to conquer the whole country, founding the city of Trinovant, New Troy, which became London, along the way. So did Albion become Britain, the land of Brutus. All subsequent kings through to Arthur were descended from him.

The narrative covers a vast period from the Bronze Age to the coming of the Saxons, most notably including the first real telling of the full story of Arthur as we would recognise it today. A lot of things surface for the first time. The character of Merlin is clearly linked with Arthur and shown to be the magical force behind him. He arranges Arthur's conception in the familiar Tintagel episode. He moves Stonehenge by sorcery from Ireland. The story of Arthur's journey to Avalon first appears. It's important to note that there's no specific naming of Glastonbury. The Grail and Joseph of Arimathea are likewise absent.

Arthur is portrayed as a mighty monarch of the status of a Charlemagne. His Britain is a major player on the world stage, the conqueror of a great empire that includes Scandinavia and France. Arthur successfully challenges the Roman emperor. There are layers of historical memory in this apparently unlikely scenario. Only a century or so before, the Viking Canute had linked Britain and Scandinavia. Much further back, the mighty Constantine had gone from Britain to become Roman emperor and other contenders had likewise sallied forth, including one Maximus who had remained a popular figure amongst the Welsh. Geoffrey had contemporary reasons for showing Arthur as continental monarch though. Such a history helped justify and ennoble the cross-channel monarchy's position and ambitions. The Saxon era was an aberration. The new rulers were the true heirs to Britain's heritage.

Shortly after beginning the *History*, Geoffrey also started work on a book of prophecies of Merlin. He completed that project, published it separately, and then incorporated it into the larger work. There's a sense of *Revelation* about its style. Geoffrey later wrote a *Life of Merlin* in which he expanded on the details of Arthur's departure to Avalon. Merlin takes him to the paradisiacal Isle of Apples where Morgan and her nine sisters dwell. He will be healed there and the implication is that he will live on in some way eternally. The *Vita Merlini* seems to be the work of some kind of adept. R J Stewart has persuasively argued for the presence of an advanced coherent cosmology and philosophy within its structure. The extent to which it can be said that Geoffrey actually composed it himself or was working from other sources is another unending debate. I tend to feel that he is a mysterious figure who perhaps made some use of visionary abilities in his work.

An astounding expansion of Arthurian material followed the publication of Geoffrey's work, continuing in full flood for about a century or so. The phenomenon did not arise out of a vacuum. The political and cultural context of the time was a major determining factor in its manifestation and needs to be examined in some detail.

Henry I died in the same year that Geoffrey of Monmouth's *History* was published. England entered into a period of great turmoil as the death of his son led to a major dispute over succession. Henry's daughter Matilda had been married at the age of eight to the German Holy Roman Emperor. When widowed at twenty three, her father summoned her back to England. Some history books will refer to her as Empress, others as Princess. Henry made his barons swear to support Matilda as his successor. With a view to strengthening the Anglo-Norman empire's French connections, he then arranged for her to marry the fourteen year old Geoffrey of Anjou who was due to become monarch of that kingdom.

When riding, Geoffrey tended to wear a sprig of bloom. He became known by the Latin designation for this, *planta genista,* which ultimately provided the name for an illustrious dynasty redolent with romance and mystery. In the family mythology an early Count of Anjou, Geoffrey Greygown, married some kind of demoness/faery woman. The legend told of her discomfort in church and habitual departure before the elevation of the host. When her husband's men one day tried to detain her, she escaped their clutches, flying with a piercing scream through an open window, never to be seen again. The couple's descendents carried demon blood. The Plantaganets were not the only family of the time of whom such tales were told but their power made the legend more imposing in the popular mind.

When Henry I died the barons soon changed their minds about Matilda and set up her cousin Stephen of Blois as King. A civil war broke out that wrecked the country. The conflict ebbed and flowed for almost twenty years. Matilda was supported by her half-brother Robert of Gloucester. He was a patron of major authors of Arthurian interest, Caradoc of Llancarfan and Henry of Huntingdon. It was round about this very period of disruption that their productions appeared. The final outcome was that Stephen remained King on the basis of acknowledging Geoffrey and Matilda's son Henry as his successor.

Prince Henry was actively involved in the succession hostilities from the age of nine. It's rather extraordinary to contemplate him leading armies in the field from his early teens. He took some significant imprints then for he spent the rest of his life engaged in such activities. On a visit to Paris at the age of sixteen Henry met the French King Louis and his wife Eleanor of Aquitaine, famous as the most beautiful woman in Europe. The couple's relationship was a difficult one and would not endure. After some typical medieval political manoeuvring in which the pope was involved, Henry and Eleanor were married. In 1154, Stephen unexpectedly died. At the age of twenty-one, the Prince became Henry II, King of England, Duke of Normandy and Aquitaine, and Count of Anjou and Maine.

The new king was undoubtedly a most extraordinary man in true regal heroic mode. Multi-lingual and scholarly, he consistently applied tremendous energy to help formulate a legal system that could justly govern his realm. He was constantly travelling and working at a frenzied pace, often spending entire days on horseback, as he dealt with administration, endless minor wars and rebellions, a bevy of mistresses and international politics. He's probably not considered to be much of a hero by the Irish though. The pope acknowledged his right to sovereignty there, sending an emerald ring as a sign of that decision. A millennia of grief resulted. The Welsh (as the Cymric tribes had come to be contemptuously called) likewise resisted him. And then there was the little matter of the murder of the Archbishop of Canterbury, Thomas Beckett, after his estrangement from Henry, followed by the King's spectacular penance involving public flogging, the kind of thing a contemporary tabloid editor can only dream about.

The marriage of Henry and Eleanor was somewhat tempestuous. At one point he kept her imprisoned. Their children included two of England's most famous kings, Richard the Lion Heart and John. As they came to adulthood, extraordinary machinations concerning honours and succession were a constant backdrop. The superb 1968 movie, *The Lion in Winter,* gives a fine sense of the spirit of the time. Peter O'Toole and Katharine Hepburn are magnificent as Henry and Eleanor. The events leading from the accession of Henry, through Richard's crusading career, to the climax of John's reign with the Magna Carta, have lingered in the collective mythic memory bank with undiminished vitality.

There's a moment in the Hollywood movie *Ivanhoe* that encapsulates it all for me. Whilst Richard is held captive abroad, the nation has suffered under the tyrant Prince John. Robin Hood and his merry men have bravely fought to see the justice of the true king prevail. Suddenly, he appears with his crusader knights. In their distinctive red cross on white surcoat uniforms they ride en-masse onto the scene. Every single time I've seen that film, from the age of ten to the present day, I get cold tingles all over when they arrive. I know he really wasn't a good king. I'm more than aware that *Ivanhoe* is mythology but it still gets to me and I'm entirely happy about that. The period has all that incredible history, romance, and mythology, before even looking at Arthur and the Grail.

The Grail Epoch

"The legends of chivalry are veiled accounts of man's eternal search for truth. These beautiful stories are not, however, merely folklore. They are parts of an orderly tradition, unfolding through the centuries and bearing witness to a well-organised plan and program. Like the myths of classical antiquity, the hero tales are sacred rituals belonging to secret Fraternities perpetuating the esoteric doctrines of antiquity."

Manly P Hall
Orders of the Quest

TWELFTH CENTURY AMBIENCE

Whilst all these events were occurring in Britain, Arthur ascended to prominence. One more element was required for his myth cycle to unleash its full potency. The Grail. William Blake's linking of Arthur with Albion helped me establish an initial perspective from which to view the confusing mix of mythic and historical details on the once and future king. An even larger overview was necessary to profitably approach the Grail stories.

A crucial distinction was made by Ouspensky in *A New Model of the Universe*. He wrote of the dynamic interplay between the principles of civilisation and barbarism that weaves its way through history. An unashamed advocate of esotericism, he claimed that, *"The beginning of culture comes from the inner circle of humanity, and often it comes by means that are violent. Missionaries of the inner circle civilise savage races sometimes by fire and sword, because there can be no other means but violence to deal with a savage people. Later the principles of civilisation develop and gradually create those forms of man's spiritual manifestation which are called religion, philosophy, science and art, and also those forms of social life which create for the individual a certain freedom, leisure, security and the possibility of self-manifestation in higher spheres of activity."*

However, *"the original forms of civilisation cultivated certain forms of barbarism for the protection of their own existence, their own defence"* and, *"these forms of barbarism very soon outgrow civilisation. Very soon they begin to see the aim of their existence in themselves. Their strength lies in the fact that they can exist by themselves, without help from outside. Civilisation, on the contrary, having come from outside can only exist and develop by receiving outside help, that is, the help of the esoteric circle. But the evolving forms of barbarism very soon cut off civilisation from its source, and then civilisation, losing confidence in the reason for its separate existence, begins to serve the developed forms of barbarism, in the belief that here lies its aim and destiny. – Civilisation is, as it were, recast in the mould of barbarism."*

Historians of art and culture refer to a twelfth century Renaissance. This was the period I came to increasingly focus upon, feeling that it manifested with mind-shattering intensity, the processes of which Ouspensky wrote. It was, briefly, a time of incredible openness and expansion when, as far as I was concerned, to use the words of Julius Evola, *"suprahistorical reality imposed itself on history"*. It wasn't long though, before a barbaric contraction had occurred and the Middle Ages of popular conception, of the Inquisition and constant terror of the devil and all his works, had set in. This was the backdrop to the Grail era.

In the early twelfth century in Paris, a remarkable blend of influences led to far-reaching developments that would later strangely resonate in Glastonbury. It had begun centuries before with the misidentification of three different figures. An obscure associate of St Paul named Dionysius the Areopagite was mixed up with a neo-platonic Gnostic tinged Christian mystical philosopher now generally known as Pseudo Dionysius. They were in turn falsely linked with the patron Saint of Paris, St Denis. All three became one individual.

A royal abbey named after the saint became the most important in Paris. The bones of saints and kings were gathered together, figures that stretched back into a mythological past. Coronations and state affairs were held there. The tales of Arthur formed a body of literature that came to be known as the Matter of Britain. There was already a Matter of France in existence and it was cultivated at the abbey of St Denis. This was centred on Charlemagne and his knights such as Roland. It served to promote national identity and the image and credibility of the French monarchy.

In 1123, one Abbot Suger took charge of the place. He was a major political figure who had served as prime minister and was closely allied with the monarchy having actually arranged and presided over the marriage of Eleanor of Aquitaine to the future King Louis.

As well as his worldly wisdom Suger was also a mystic, moved by the

writings attributed to the saint of Paris. Dionysius is an often underestimated figure of tremendous importance in the western mystery tradition.
He is probably best known for his classification of nine orders or choirs of
angels into seraphim and cherubim etc. He praised the virtues of divine
names. There are many points of similarity with Qabalistic teachings. He
later influenced Renaissance magi who in turn inspired the Golden Dawn. In
the twentieth century Rudolf Steiner made much of his angelic hierarchies.
Most importantly to Abbot Suger, Dionysius extolled the divine light, God's
holy fire that animates the entire universe. 'Lux continua,' continuous light,
became Suger's ultimate metaphor for God. To be purified, illuminated and
perfected in divine light seemed the ultimate mysticism.

The abbot wanted to rebuild the existing church in a spectacular manner
that would make it the wonder of Europe. It would be constructed to present
the teachings of Paris' patron saint to the world, to lead people to the divine
light. Nine chapels in the eastern apse and a further nine in the crypt would
call to mind the nine orders of angels. The decoration would evoke the
city of the New Jerusalem. By 1133, Suger had assembled an international
team of artists and craftsmen, including Arabic glass-makers. The whole style
of the building, including the first major appearance of huge coloured
stained glass windows in Europe was an event of significant cultural impact.
Suger referred to it as an 'opus modernum,' a modern work. In terms of
its effects on people's consciousness, the new multi-media art-form with
its synaesthetic blending of space, light, colour, sound, and smell in the
interaction of building and ritual would be the LSD of the day. It was very
much a case of the shock of the new. The medium was a vital aspect of
the message.

This prototype Gothic cathedral was finished in 1144. It's an irony of
cultural history that the term 'Gothic' was never used by the people of the
time. It arose hundreds of years later in a critical backlash that derided
the style as barbaric. The term has endured and its negative connotations
dissolved. The dedication ceremony at St Denis was attended by many
leading figures of the age, including the royal couple Louis VII and Eleanor
of Aquitaine, a multi-national host of bishops, a vast throng of nobility, and
the top ecclesiastical superstar of the time, Bernard of Clairvaux.

One extraordinary artefact was a notable centrepiece for the dazzling
bejewelled edifice. A sardonyx cup, now considered to have originated in
Alexandria during the second to first centuries BC, was incorporated into a
gold and silver chalice adorned with gems. It was used to hold wine for Mass
and had featured in Eleanor's coronation. The Suger chalice (now in the
National Gallery of Art in Washington) is one of the minor contenders in the

cup of Christ relic stakes. What's interesting here is that such an item, regardless of its true provenance, was a focal point of such a richly realised cosmological vision in stone and glass, the main model for a whole culture that followed. From its beginnings at St Denis, the new style soon spread all over Europe.

During the first millennium of the Catholic Church the central Mass rite of the Eucharist was not yet finalised. It had evolved from what appears to have been a commemorative meal expressive of group communion and solidarity. At the beginning of the Gothic Grail era, the form of the ceremony was still developing. Many tales were also circulating at the time of the romances of people being sustained solely by the Eucharistic host. It was at the end of the twelfth century that elements such as the elevation of the host and the ringing of bells became commonplace. Performance in the new cathedrals and churches would have seemed intense and dramatic. The mysterious rite was conducted amidst candles and incense by people in striking costumes. Not everyone had believed in transubstantiation, the real presence of Christ, that the Mass wine and wafer was his blood and body. This became official doctrine at the Fourth Lateran Council of 1215. It helped enforce papal power throughout Western Europe. Only the officially sanctioned could perform it. Any deviance was heresy and subject to increasingly grim punishment.

In 1141, a mystically inclined nun named Hildegard of Bingen in Germany had an experience when, *"a burning light of tremendous brightness coming from heaven poured into my entire mind, like a flame that does not burn but enkindles. It inflamed my entire heart and breast, like the sun that warms an object with its rays."* This and future visions contained images, voices, and strangely floating written words that formed the basis of a forty year long out-pouring of art, theology, prophecy, medicine, and above all, music, that made her one of the wonders of the age, chastiser of corrupt priests, the confidante of common folk and the Holy Roman Emperor. Hildegard was a very real example of the presence and potency of the experience of divine light that was inspiring the Gothic cathedral building. The fact that she was a woman who managed to make her voice heard and accepted also says something about the spirit of the time.

The great cathedrals that were appearing all over Europe were primarily dedicated to the Virgin Mary whose cult was massively expanded by their success. Bernard of Clairvaux was a major figure in the initial process. He was another incredible balance of politician and mystic. The Cistercian order of monks had been rescued by him from floundering fortunes and transformed into one of the most dynamic multi-national corporations of the day. Bernard had inaugurated the Second Crusade in 1146 in France, preaching to a football stadium sized crowd that included Louis and Eleanor. A less successful undertaking was a mission to the heretical Cathars. Bernard interacted with all of the major game-players of the age. There is correspondence between him and Hildegard. He was primarily a mystic. A childhood experience, difficult to classify today, when he received some drops of milk from a statue of the Virgin Mary, produced a lifelong veneration. The statue in question was one of the enigmatic Black Madonnas. Bernard went on to write a prodigious number of sermons linking the Virgin to material in the Old Testament Song of Songs, a piece full of the erotic and mystical divine feminine, characterised as black. After Suger initiated the Gothic epoch at St Denis, Bernard was a prime mover behind the greatest masterpiece of esoteric architecture that followed soon afterwards. Built on what was once a major Druidic site, Chartres cathedral has spawned a whole industry of interpretation. What's not in dispute is the central importance of a Black Madonna statue originally displayed in a crypt there.

Joachim of Fiore was an abbot obsessed with potential hidden meanings in the Bible. Sometime between 1190 and 1195 he came to conclusions that would make him the most important of all medieval visionaries, an influence across an astonishingly diverse spectrum right through into the present day. He believed that history was intricately linked to the unfolding of god's plan for humanity. It was divided into three ages that were presided over by the Father, Son and Holy Spirit. There had been 42 generations between Adam and Christ, the first age of the Father. He believed that another 42 would complete the era of the Son. The glorious epoch of the Holy Spirit would then descend. As Norman Cohn summarised it in *The Pursuit of the Millennium,* "*If the first age had been one of fear and servitude and the second age one of faith and filial submission, the third age would be one of love, joy and freedom, when the knowledge of God would be revealed directly in the hearts of all men.*"

There was a time of overlap between the ages. Joachim believed that the first stirrings of the age of the Holy Spirit would be clearly felt by 1260. After his death in 1202 assorted false writings were attributed to him. The incredible subsequent history of his ideas need not concern us here. Sufficient to note that the idea of three ages, "*entered into the common stock of European social mythology*" and some mystics and heretics would come to feel the imminence of the age of the Spirit.

The same spiritual cultural influences and conditions that produced the building of the Gothic cathedrals, the massive expansion of the cult of the Virgin Mary, the debate about the Eucharist, a divine light download in a visionary nun, and led a mystic to believe that the age of the Holy Spirit was about to dawn, were also present in the creation of the Grail literature.

When it comes to the great tales themselves, it can be useful to begin with the perspective of the German medievalist Friedrich Heer. *"There can no longer be any doubt that the theme of the great romantic epics — is initiation, dedication, metamorphosis, and absorption into a higher and fuller life, at once more human and more divine".* Enter the mystery with that attitude and the ambience of the twelfth century all around one and the journey can be a most fruitful one.

CHRETIEN

One work has been generally considered to be the point of origin. In about 1180, Chretien de Troyes produced *Le Conte du Graal* (the story of the Grail), or *Perceval* as it's often known. The author had a background in the classics and was already an acclaimed writer of romances featuring Arthurian characters. He claimed that his patron Phillip of Flanders gave him a book containing a story that he wanted developed. Chretien's tale tells how the innocent Perceval leaves his widowed mother and wanders into the world of which he knows next to nothing in search of adventure. He eventually becomes one of Arthur's knights. In a mysterious castle, he encounters a richly dressed wounded man languishing on a couch. This is the Fisher King whose land is imperilled through his inability to properly govern it.

Perceval then witnesses bizarre events that have inspired and perplexed multitudes in the centuries since. The Fisher King presents him with a sword. A procession then enters the room, headed by a young man carrying a lance whose tip drips blood. He is followed by two more young men, bearing candelabra aflame with light. They are accompanied by a beautiful young woman holding a golden bejewelled light radiating 'Grail'. A further damsel brings up the rear, carrying a silver dish. The strange group are a prelude to a great meal served only to Perceval and the Fisher King. The innocent youth had been instructed in discretion so, despite his curiosity and desire to ask questions, he keeps silent during the proceedings. He later discovers that this was a great error. If he had simply asked the Fisher King what was going on, it would have been sufficient to heal him of his condition. When Perceval awakes in the morning, the castle is deserted. He leaves the place sorely puzzled by what he has seen.

Twelfth century Europe was rife with heresy. Chretien's patron was a known heretic buster. It is understandable that many have detected hints of some secret sect in the haunting Grail scene. A ceremony seems to be depicted. There is not a single representative of the Church present. The most significant object is borne by a woman. A number of strange groups arose in France featuring female incarnations of the principle of Sapientia, Sophia, Gnosis, Wisdom, the divine light that can bring humanity closer to God. It is not out of the question that some of these women may have been having similar experiences to Hildegard of Bingen who can readily be seen as a Sophianic figure. Such cults walked a road of excess that often led to violent death.

The Fisher King's father is sustained solely by a host served from the Grail. This strange figure appears briefly. As Leonardo Olschki observed in his classic study, *The Grail Castle and Its Mysteries, "it is the Grail, and not a liturgical act, that consecrates the host and confers miraculous powers upon it to the extent of affording physical and spiritual nourishment to a penitent ascetic"* who *"seems to personify the ideal figure of those who desire to attain superhuman perfection without the aid of the liturgy and ecclesiastical guidance."* In this, he has something in common with the most famous world-rejecting heretics of the time, the Cathars.

Another angle of insight on Chretien came from Professor Urban T Holmes. There was a notable Qabalistic Rabbinical school in Troyes. Holmes believed that Chretien was a converted Jew and the Grail castle a symbol of Solomon's Temple. The Fisher King is depicted wearing a robe fringed with purple which seems to carry an echo of a requirement of Mosaic law featured in *Numbers XV38*. He also seems to be wearing a kind of skull cap. Excalibur is linked to Aaron's rod which could only be pulled from the ground by Moses. During the Feast of Passover the youngest member of a family is required to ask what the significance of the night is. Holmes links this with the necessity of questioning the Fisher King on the function of the Grail. There is also the motif of the Perilous Seat, the chair left empty at Arthur's round table for the Grail winner. At Jewish circumcision feasts, a place at the table is prepared and left empty for the possible appearance of Elijah. As we shall see, there were a few other people with an interest in Solomon's Temple working from the Troyes vicinity at the time, so that leaves a Templar connection as a possibility.

Chretien's story was unfinished. It appears that he died before completing it. Nonetheless it seems to be leading ultimately in an orthodox direction as Perceval learns about the church from a hermit. One interpretation suggests that it presents an archetypal mish-mash simply representing 'heresy' per se as a warning. If this is true, Chretien has set about his task in a strange manner by portraying the Grail ceremony in a positive way and not criticising it. The author's true intentions remain tantalisingly obscure.

CONTINUATION AND CHRISTIANISATION

A number of other writers took up the tale in a series of 'continuations'. It does not necessarily follow that all authors of Grail romances were initiates of some kind or were following an esoteric agenda. Many of them were fed ideas and given general plot instructions by assorted patrons who may well have had unusual motivations but there was scope for expression of individual creativity and this should not be underestimated as a factor in the total blend. Not every detail of a story can be unravelled to reveal an all-encompassing key.

Some version of the Grail procession and feast became an essential feature in the literature. The details of what appear to be ritual objects (that came to be known as the Grail Hallows) varied. Chretien doesn't actually specify the form of his Grail. It is not clearly identified as a chalice. He also refers to it as *'un graal'*, meaning *a* rather than *the* Grail, implying they exist in the plural. A number of early romances say the Grail is a dish, usually the one used at the Last Supper. The chalice eventually became the generally accepted form. What the various versions do have in common is the depiction of bright light as the most obvious sign of the Grail's presence.

The Joseph of Arimathea mythos finally appears in written form somewhere between 1199 and 1212 in the work of Robert de Borron. It is with him that the Grail story receives a strong Christianisation that has endured ever since. He was the first author to focus on the Grail itself rather than the knights who quested for it. *L' Estoire dou Grail*, The History of the Grail, was conceived as a kind of trilogy that would in turn deal with the Joseph of Arimathea story, the advent of Merlin and Arthur, and finally, the already familiar Perceval tale.

The Joseph section has a style akin to biographies of saints and apocryphal gospels rather than romance literature. Joseph used the dish from the Last Supper to collect blood from the crucified Christ as he was laid out in his tomb. The Jews imprisoned him without food for his support of the false messiah. Christ manifested the Grail for him in his cell. Somehow it kept him alive for forty years. On release from prison he left Palestine with his sister Enygeus, her husband Bron, and a group of newly converted Jews, to preach the Gospel in other lands. The timing of the tale corresponds to the calamitous events of 70 AD, when the great Jewish revolt was crushed, the Temple destroyed, and the entire population dispersed.

As the story unfolds, Bron becomes the next keeper of the Grail and becomes known as the Fisher King. When Merlin asks Uther Pendragon to found the Round Table it completes a sequence of three. The first was that of the Last Supper. The second was one that Joseph and his group eat from as part of a redemptive meal after their crops had failed through sin. Perceval gets a second chance to ask the vital question and Bron is cured of his sickness. A number of elements vital to the developing mythos have been established. The Round Table has been clearly linked with the table of the Last Supper. Arthur's knights, through Perceval, have a family relationship to Joseph of Arimathea. In order for this aspect of the narrative to hang together, the Arimathean family have to live as long as Old Testament patriarchs.

It's worth noting that Joseph was becoming a figure of increasing signifi-cance at the time in the context of the evolving Eucharist that reached its final form in 1215. The elements of the Mass were interpreted allegorically. The deacon who put a covered chalice on the altar was linked to Joseph who had put a shroud over the body of Christ in the tomb. De Borron makes much of the Eucharistic interests of the day. When Christ manifests the Grail for Joseph in his cell, an explanation of the Mass is expounded in the familiar symbolism of the altar cloth representing the shroud and so on. The Grail is the cup of the Last Supper. The Grail ceremony is clearly a Eucharistic rite. Some had theorised that not only was the bread and wine transformed into flesh and blood but the chalice used actually became in that instant one and the same with the original used at the last supper. Such ideas would have needed to be treated very carefully after the 1215 ruling.

During this period the Church kept silent on the subject of the Grail with one exception. A Cistercian chronicler named Helinandus wrote of a hermit who, in the year 717 AD was granted a vision through the help of an angel. He saw Joseph of Arimathea and the vessel used in the Last Supper, a wide deep saucer plate. This vision inspired the monk to write a Latin book. Helinandus said he had seen an incomplete form of the work in French. This curious tempting fragment has been dated to around 1202 although there are the usual disagreements with cases made for a decade or so later. It does seem to suggest yet another now vanished strand of tradition.

Forty years or so after Chretien a group of romances appeared that all featured Lancelot as the central character and were linked in ongoing narrative sequence. *History of the Holy Grail, Merlin, Lancelot, Quest of the Holy Grail,* and the *Death of Arthur* were the main sources for the late medieval Malory and, through him, the Victorian Tennyson's works.

Quest features a full depiction of a scene that has become archetypal. At Whitsun, the feast of Pentecost, commemorating the descent of the Holy Spirit upon the Apostles as tongues of fire, Arthur and his knights are gathered around their famous table. There is a clap of thunder and a blinding sunbeam that illuminates the whole place. All are struck dumb as the Grail enters, covered with white samite, borne by some invisible being. The hall is infused with heavenly fragrance and somehow all are fed their favourite food. Leaving such comprehensive fulfilment, the Grail departs in a manner none can understand. The knights pledge to quest for it from that moment on. Here indeed a visionary writer seems to have tapped into the zeitgeist that also inspired Joachim of Fiore to produce a vision of a potential dawning of the age of the Holy Spirit.

INTERPRETATIONS

So far there are definite hints of strange influences but still within a Christian context. We've already seen how the heavily Celtic tales of Arthur found their way into Norman and then European consciousness. The Grail stories also contain elements of the same Celtic package that followed a similar route. The hallows can be found in Irish tales. The Tuatha De Danaan had four treasures: the Stone of Destiny, a spear, sword, and the inexhaustible cauldron of the God Dagda. This kind of cauldron features in Arthur's early *Spoils of Annwn* adventure. The assorted Grail knights appear to be solar heroes of some kind. They undergo very similar adventures. They are associated with a spear, a sword, a hawk, and some kind of sacred inexhaustible vessel. It's commonly held that the name of Lancelot derives from Lugh, the Celtic God of light. Gawain seems to derive from the Welsh Gwalchmei, meaning Hawk of May. Galahad may come from Gwalch-Haved, the Summer Hawk, Son of the Spear of Light. The Welsh form of Perceval, Peredur connects to Paladr-Hir, 'He of the Spear'. This represents only the surface of the vast amount of Celtic material present in the Grail tale narratives. Many enthusiasts have considered it to be the central core of the mythos.

It does seem though that some fruitful comparative data can be found by looking further afield. Lewis Spence compared Arthur with Egyptian Osiris. After being killed by his treacherous brother Set, Osiris was taken on a boat across the Nile by the mourning sisters Isis and Nepthys to a western paradisiacal land of bountiful fruit and grain, to reign as a lord of departed souls and await his resurrection. The Nile was identified with Osiris. He was known as Lord of the Fish in this aspect. At a certain stage in its inundation the river becomes red with soil, considered to be the blood of Osiris and this stimulated the fertility of the land in a Grail-type manner. The role of Mordred, Arthur's departure with the ladies on the vessel to Avalon the otherworld western apple isle and the promise of return, seem to rather strongly echo the Egyptian story.

Rudolf Steiner stated that, *"Fundamentally speaking, the phrase the 'Holy Grail', with all that it entails, means the reappearance of the essence of the eastern mysteries."* Mystery cults were a vital part of religious life throughout the ancient world. They included both public ceremonials and more selective initiations focused on seasonal dramas of death and resurrection featuring gods and goddesses. Deities such as Sumero-Babylonian Tammuz and the Phoenician-Greek Adonis are examples of beings intimately linked with the seasonal drama, veritable vegetation deities, infused with the spirit of life. Adonis was wounded in the thigh by a wild boar and died. He was loved by Aphrodite who arranged for him to spend only half of the year in the underworld. These cults sometimes featured feasts where special mixing-bowl cups known as kraters carried sacramental liquids now considered to have been probably psycho-active. GRS Mead and Jung both mentioned the possibility of links between the classical krater and the Grail.

JG Frazer's epochal epic *The Golden Bough* had collected together vast amounts of data from the world's religious history and folklore pertinent to these themes. He came to feel that much of it demonstrated a fundamental belief that the king and the land are one. The vegetation deity lives within him, so the monarch's vitality is linked to the fertility of the earth. When he is healthy the crops thrive, when he declines, the land does with him. As a result, he may have to be ritually killed by a healthy successor.

Something about all this reminded Arthurian scholar Jessie Weston of the recurring theme of the wasteland in the Grail tales. The Fisher King seems to be a Frazerian monarch in decline. His mysterious wounding through the thighs is often taken as a euphemism for impotence. The whole kingdom suffers with him. In *From Ritual to Romance,* published in 1920, she argued that romance literature derived from myth, and because Frazer believed that myth derived from ritual, romance literature could have some kind of foundation in ancient ritual.

Jessie Weston, using Frazer as her inspiration, whilst not ignoring the Celtic sources, also sought additional roots far more widely, coming to the inspiring hypothesis that there may have been a direct continuity linking ancient fertility rites with the Grail romances. Something of the classical mystery cults lingered. The Christian connection could have been cultivated by Gnostic groups during the early centuries AD before they were suppressed. Jesus could be seen as the ultimate dying and resurrected mystery cult deity. There may well be greater links between early Christianity and the old cults than the later churches were willing to admit. Some kind of sect may have lingered and the procession and artefacts seen by Perceval could be a glimpse of their workings.

Weston's theories don't have much credibility amongst Arthurian scholars today but their cultural impact has been significant. TS Eliot's *The Wasteland* was one of the most important poems of the twentieth century. Its structure was shaped by *From Ritual to Romance*. My own favourite movie, *Apocalypse Now*, has many levels of narrative. Hints of its depths come when Colonel Kurtz's book collection is shown to contain Weston. He himself is a Fisher King figure in the midst of a wasteland, and knows it. The "King and the land are one" theme was also used to great effect in *Excalibur*.

The romances seem to suggest an alternative apostolic succession to the Catholic Church. The Biblical Peter was a fisherman. The *New Testament* suggests that he was the cornerstone, the rock on which the Church was founded. Each subsequent pope fills the 'shoes of the fisherman'. Might the Fisher King be an alternative pope? The Grail, whatever it may be, is almost always a relic of the first Mass, the Last Supper. It's not entrusted to St Peter but to Joseph of Arimathea. If the man really went off and founded his own church can we spot it on the pages of real history? In *The Chalice of the Magdalene*, Graham Phillips has wondered if the heresy known as Pelagianism may offer a clue. It flourished in the last days of Roman Britain and questioned the apostolic succession of the Catholic Church. The pope sent a heresy-buster to Britain to sort it all out. St Germanus preached to the British chieftain Vortigern, implying he was a Pelagian. This is very near to the time of Arthur. No surviving sources ever mention Joseph though. It may well be one of the minor wonders of the Kali Yuga that the Pelagian heresy would eventually feature as a significant plot-device in the 2004 Hollywood film *King Arthur*, perhaps a measure of the power of the dragon king to still produce surprises.

HERMETIC PARZIVAL

The most famous of all the Grail romances, Wolfram von Eschenbach's *Parzival* was certainly written before 1220, when the author died. 1200-1210 is the general consensus. The story does seem to contain influences from entirely different sources than the other works of the time that lend themselves readily to esoteric interpretations.

Parzival was dynamically and controversially re-energised by Wagner. If Trevor Ravenscroft's *Spear of Destiny* can be trusted, the young Adolf Hitler was a profound student of the arcane depths of the text. Walter Johannes Stein certainly believed that *Parzival* was full of esoterica and produced his extraordinary work, *The Ninth Century* to support his theory

that the characters were based on specific historical individuals from a few
centuries earlier. Otto Rahn in *Crusade Against the Grail* rooted the story
firmly in the Cathar territory of southern France. In *The Sign and the Seal*
Graham Hancock drew the attention of a wider audience to Wolfram with his
hypothesis that the text held clues to the presence of the Ark of the Covenant
in Ethiopia. It's a rare work of literature that can stimulate such diverse
thought eight hundred years after its creation.

Wolfram criticises Chretien, boasting that he has the correct story. He
got it from Kyot, a Troubadour from Provence, who had found the tale
written in Arabic by Flegetanis, a Jewish astrologer of some kind in Toledo
who *"saw with his own eyes in the constellations things he was shy to talk
about, hidden mysteries. He said there was a thing called the Grail, whose
name he had read in the constellations." "A host left it on earth and then flew
away up over the stars."* There are two basic positions concerning Kyot He
is either a fictional device or a real historical individual functioning in the
midst of heresy.

In Wolfram's version the Grail is not a chalice or platter, but a green stone
fallen from heaven during the Luciferic rebellion and once guarded by
the angels who had been neutral in that conflict. By the power of this *lapsit
exillis*, the phoenix is burnt to ashes and then reborn from them. Health and
youth can be bestowed upon humans who see it. On one day of the year,
Good Friday, the dove of the holy spirit comes to rest upon it and the stone
is able to provide, *"the best food and drink in the world."*

'Lapsit exillis' may be the most debated words in the whole Arthurian
corpus. Perhaps it means 'stone from heaven'. Maybe it doesn't really mean
anything in itself but refers to something else that looks very similar. The
usual candidate is *Lapis Elixir*, the Philosopher's Stone of alchemy. Given
the nature and properties of Wolfram's Grail, this seems a reasonable theory.
The angelically guarded stone calls to mind the Meccan Ka'aba.

The most fruitful speculation on Wolfram may perhaps be found in
The Krater and the Grail: Hermetic Sources of the Parzival by Henry and
Renee Kahanne. What is Hermeticism? In the early centuries AD, Alexandria
surpassed Rome as a multi-cultural centre. People from all over the empire
and beyond gathered there. Its gigantic library was legendary. Indian
'Gymnosophists' and Persian Magi met with Jewish Mystics, Greek
philosophers, Egyptian magicians and Gnostic Christians in a climate of
cross-fertilisation and tolerance. Works from the ancient cult centres of
Babylon and Assyria were available for inspection. Extraordinary mixtures
resulted. Much of the foundations of the whole western magical tradition were
laid there. Beliefs that later resurfaced during the Renaissance and in the

Golden Dawn can be traced back to the fabulous matrix of Alexander's city. The Egyptian god Thoth and the Greek Hermes had become identified with each other. They were both associated with communication between the human and divine realms, and with writing and magic. The figure of Hermes Trismegistus, the thrice-great, emerged from this. He came to be seen as someone who had lived as a human being but been divinely inspired to reveal mysteries to the human race. In some versions, he attains immortality. A number of authors wrote works in his name, which are collectively known as the *Corpus Hermeticum*, on mystical, magical and philosophical themes, often featuring Egyptian deities. They tend to emphasise the harmony and inter-relationship between all of creation. The mysterious art and science of alchemy also developed from the same mix of influences.

Between the triumph of Christianity, with its subsequent library, book, and heretic burning, and a fifteenth century Renaissance revival, there's a period of about a thousand years where the whole thing seems at first glance to have disappeared. The usual story tells how, after the fall of Constantinople to the Ottoman Turks in 1453, scholars from the old Byzantine Empire brought previously unavailable books to the west. Part of this process enabled Marsilio Ficino to translate Hermetic works for Cosimo de Medici. This material had a massive influence on the Renaissance. A case can be made for Hermeticism being *the* major impetus behind it. The art of Botticelli, for example, seems to be suffused with its inspiration. Is it at all feasible that any such material may have influenced the Grail literature?

Hermetic literature could have arrived from the Byzantine Empire much earlier than 1453. The Neoplatonic scholar Michael Psellus is known to have had various texts in his possession in Constantinople around 1050 AD. The Fourth Crusade in 1204 had ended in an ignominious debacle when the knights en-route to the Holy Land, having graciously been allowed passage through Byzantine territory, let their greed overcome them when confronted by the fabulous wealth of Constantinople. They sacked the place, carrying treasures back to Europe in a manner later perfected by Hermann Goering. Saintly relics and assorted esoteric oddities were amongst the booty. The presence of Hermetica amongst it is by no means impossible.

One of the works within the *Corpus Hermeticum* is called the *Krater,* sometimes translated as simply, *The Cup.* The text takes the form of a discourse given by Hermes to his pupil Tat who interjects with questions. *"Tell me then, father, why did God not impart intellect to all men? - It was his will, my son, that intellect should be placed in the midst as a prize that human souls may win. - And where did he place it? - He filled a great Krater with intellect, and sent it down to earth; and he appointed a herald, and bade him make proclamation to the hearts of men "Dip yourself in this Krater, you who are able; you who believe that you will ascend to him who sent this Krater down. – Now they who gave heed to the proclamation and were baptised in intellect, those men got a share of gnosis."*

By intellect is meant not simply the human faculty of rational thinking but the Greek word *Nous*, the very Mind of God. The Krater symbolises the Monad, the ultimate oneness of the divine from which flows an endless outpouring in which a conscious baptism may be possible. Michael Psellus commented on the Hermetic *Krater* text clearly equating Nous with the Holy Spirit of Christianity. The wafer bearing dove of Wolfram could easily be seen as an image of Nous.

In the wider culture of the time the Krater was usually linked with the constellation of the same name. The classical writer Macrobius saw it as a cosmic halfway house where souls coming down into physical incarnation drunk from the bowl of Bacchus and were rendered intoxicated and forgetful in the manner of Gnostic myths which tell of humanity having forgotten its divine origins. Other texts such as the Gnostic *Pistis Sophia* speak of cups given to the soul between incarnations that may induce forgetfulness or an agitation to induce the future body to pine for the divine. These vessels have a heavenly origin in common.

For the Kahannes, *"Hermetism's krater then, is the same as Wolfram's gral: the symbol around which a select ethico-religious brotherhood gathers."* They even put forward a complex etymological argument that derives the very word Grail from the classical Krater. The obvious problem is that Wolfram's Grail is usually thought of as a stone. The theory is advanced that the *stein* of Wolfram is initially used in a context that echoes a section in the Hermetic *Krater* where, after a glimpse of God, the sight attracts the soul toward the divine like a magnetic lodestone. The *Parzival* stone is a metaphor for the Grail and says nothing of its true form. Chretien's Perceval receives teachings about religion of which he had been ignorant from a hermit. This figure becomes far more developed in Wolfram in the form of the magus-like Trevrizent. The Kahannes believe his name derives from Hermes' epithet 'thrice greatest'.

Wolfram portrays a procession and feast far more elaborate than Chretien's. Twenty five ladies appear in a sequential set of groupings that the Kahannes ingeniously interpret as representative of a Hermetic cosmology that shows the journey of the soul towards the divine. The first four women are the four elements. They are followed by eight celestial spheres, twelve signs of the zodiac, and finally, the Grail bearer, the Monad, the ultimate One.

Each group also carries a number of lights that *"may well represent the constituents of the soul in its various phases on the way back to God."* In the first instance, the four physical elements are balanced by spiritual elements of soul and intellect so four ladies, two lights. It works its way up through a Gnostic Qabalistic-style schemata until all is unified in the one light.

In *Lord of the World,* the French esotericist Rene Guenon has further suggestions on the Grail as green stone enigma. *"This emerald strongly recalls the 'urna' or Hindu frontal jewel (subsequently adopted by Buddhists). It usually depicts the place of the third eye of Shiva, representing what can be called the 'sense of eternity'.* The astonishing autobiography of the modern Indian adept Swami Muktananda, *Play of Consciousness,* describes a yogic kundalini process leading to a supreme attainment known as the vision of the blue pearl, symbol of the supreme self, of Shiva. It does seem to parallel many elements of the Grail literature.

Innumerable examples throughout the medieval romances tell of assorted ecstasies in terms that seem descriptive of physiological processes. When the eastern mystics talk of enlightenment they know that the yogic techniques can induce experiences of overwhelming light, the most often reported sign of the presence of the Grail. This light may be felt as permeating the whole body-mind, producing swooning trances of love-bliss. The terminology of the time would speak of the recipient being filled with the Holy Spirit. The Grail seems to be infinitely nourishing. Some are fed what they most desire until they lose all need of food. It heals wounds and prolongs life.

On the path to such fulfilments there may be problems. The accounts of knights who are blinded, lose the use of their limbs, or are burnt to a cinder when approaching the Grail in an unprepared and unworthy state, may be indications of what the eastern adepts would recognise as signs of a prematurely or wrongly awakened kundalini. In Malory, Lancelot sees the blinding Grail light and hears a voice warning him to go no further. He carries on regardless and is hit in the face by a fire, collapsing and losing all control of his limbs. Some around him think he has died but an old man comments that he, *"has more life in him than the strongest among you."* Lancelot remains in an apparently catatonic state for twenty four days, eventually awakening to tell of the bliss he has experienced.

Wolfram's Grail Castle is named 'Monsalvaesche' which is often taken to mean, 'the mountain of salvation'. The model for this citadel has been variously located at the Cathar stronghold of Montsegur in southern France and even a Manichean centre, the Ruh-I-Sal-Shwadeha, at Lake Hamun on the border between Iran and Afghanistan. After his initial failure to ask the right question Parzival does return and get it right. In this instance it's because the name of the Grail winner sometimes can be seen written on the stone and spells out Parzival's name at the feast. He becomes the new monarch of the rejuvenated kingdom.

All kinds of angles of enquiry present themselves through the Monsalvaesche comparative data and the hints of hidden historical links they may suggest. The most enigmatic Grail mountain material can be found through the study of another German romance. Like Chretien, Wolfram left a tale unfinished. His *Titurel* was significantly elaborated upon by Albrecht von Scharfenberg into what's generally known as *Later Titurel*, perhaps the last classic Grail tale of that epoch.

The author lavishes 112 lines on a wealth of detail. The Grail temple is set on top of a mountain made of onyx, with the earth on the summit cleared and the stone polished to shine like a mirror. The temple was high and circular with a domed roof. Around the edge were twenty-two chapel-type areas laid out on an octagonal design. The interior ceiling was enamelled to represent the sky. A gold sun and silver moon were moved mechanically around as cymbals sounded to mark the rhythm of the heavenly bodies. The central area was surrounded by twenty-two arches. There were doors on three sides of the building. The entire place was filled with bejewelled finery and decoration.

It was only in the twentieth century that scholars realised there are distinctive similarities between Albrecht's Grail temple and a forgotten historical location. In the seventh century AD, King Chosroes II of Sassanian Persia constructed a temple palace on a mountain already sacred to the ancient fire-venerating faith of Zoroastrianism as a reputed birthplace of its founder. The kings of his time took part in seasonal ceremonies there to ensure the fertility of the land. The new building, known as the Takt-i-Taqdis, the Throne of Arches, was elaborate in the extreme. It was golden domed with an interior ceiling representing the sky. Twenty-two arches encircled it. Astronomical charts containing jewels were displayed.

The entire building was constructed over a huge pit whereby teams of horses were able to gradually rotate it to enable the temple to function as a permanently aligned observatory. A central area was created by twenty-two arches. The temple could only be approached from three directions. A large lake was located immediately adjacent to the building. Around the side of it was a crusty deposit resulting from mineral content of the water. It gleamed in sunlight like onyx.

Great historical drama surrounded the short life of the incredible edifice. Chosroes had waged war on the Byzantine Empire. In 614 AD he captured Jerusalem and made off with a relic believed to be part of the True Cross.

It was installed in the Takt-i-Taqdis. In 629 the vengeful Byzantines defeated the king, regained the relic, and destroyed the temple. The event was certainly a big deal at the time and was written about. Accounts circulated and became elaborated but it was seven hundred years before Albrecht's *Titurel*. It does rather seem that he had detailed knowledge of the temple. There are scholarly dissenters to that view but if we are prepared to accept the possibility then some strand of transmission other than the general influences accepted in the literature was surely present and shaped his intentions.

If all this esoterica is really contained within early medieval German works of literature, with the likelihood that similar productions of the time were likewise influenced, the obvious question is how on earth did these ideas find their way from Alexandria and beyond to Europe and why would authors want to secretly portray them? What possible routes and processes of transmission can be discerned? Are there any fellow travellers who can be potentially identified?

THE TEMPLAR CATHEDRAL ENIGMA

The big political picture of the time is strongly dominated by the crusades. Jerusalem was captured on the First Crusade and a European Christian king installed. Shortly after that, in 1118, nine French knights led by Hugh de Payens came forward offering to protect pilgrim routes to the holy city. They were given royal approval and set up with a headquarters on the location where Solomon's Temple had once stood. There was something absurd about nine men being expected to protect a large territory from numerous enemies. They weren't exactly seen to be exerting themselves to that end either, for they barely ventured beyond the temple site. For the first nine years of their existence no efforts seem to have been made to find new recruits. Nonetheless, all their expenses were met and in 1128, after a synod at Troyes, the pope gave an official ruling acknowledging them as a Holy Order for their guarding of pilgrims. Such was the mysterious origin of the fabled Knights Templar. They rapidly became the most powerful military order in Europe and an international banking organisation.

What the Templars were really doing in Jerusalem has been the subject of unending speculation. Clearly the Temple of Solomon was of great significance to them. They took their name from it. Cartographers of the time placed Jerusalem at the centre of the world. The temple had been at the centre of the city. The nine knights were working at the very heart of the world. The mythology of Freemasonry has asserted that the Craft lineage can be traced back through the Templars to the days of Solomon's Temple. The dimensions of that edifice demonstrated the art and science of esoteric sacred architecture in its highest form. It's interesting to realise that it wasn't a particularly large structure, barely a hundred feet long. The general population didn't come and worship there. It was conceived as the house of god. The later, far larger, temple of Herod, where Jesus got angry at the money-changers, was built over the site of Solomon's earlier structure. In 70 AD, at the climax of the Jewish revolt, it had been destroyed along with the whole of Jerusalem. Many have believed that the Templars were searching for esoteric treasure and may have been involved in some kind of archaeological dig beneath their Temple Mount base. If they were, they were likely to have felt they had good reasons to do so. Their sponsors would probably have been in on the game to be willing to maintain funding.

The most obvious potential treasure was the Ark of the Covenant. Solomon's Temple was virtually constructed solely to house it. Hugh de Payens had visited the Holy Land with the Count of Champagne in 1104 and then again alone, in 1116. He surely must have come in contact with some sort of ideas or information that motivated his Templar enterprise. In *The Sign and the Seal,* Graham Hancock has plausibly speculated that it may have been Jewish stories that the Ark had been hidden directly beneath Solomon's Temple at the time of the Babylonian conquest, when it seemed to disappear from history. The general consensus is that the Templars didn't find it, but their subsequent meteoric ascendancy suggests that they may well have discovered something of unique value.

Masons claim that Solomon's architectural secrets lie behind the Gothic cathedrals. It does seem to be intriguingly co-incidental that the massive cathedral building epoch began at the same time as the rise of the Templars. On the most simple level, one of the most distinctive features of the new style, pointed arches, could well have been inspired by Islamic models encountered in the Holy Land. Graham Hancock believes the Templars may have found treatises on sacred architecture and building techniques that were subtly released to a select few for maximum esoteric and cultural impact. There's no doubting their advanced skills in church and castle construction. Contemporary accounts marvel at their use of vaults, arches and soaring roofs, features that also characterise Gothic architecture.

The nineteenth century saw a fashion amongst critics that has not yet fully abated whereby the idea that some kind of metaphysical geometry was a vital component of the architecture of the Gothic cathedrals was denigrated. Only the most practical aspects of geometry necessary for construction were present. If such elements could be used to express something else then fine.

Nothing else was involved. As for some of the strange decorations, gargoyles, green men and so on, they were just the meaningless playful jests of the craftsmen. Some dissenting opinions were present though. The romantic might perhaps be willing to entertain the idea that the spirit of the great cathedrals revived in accordance with some mysterious greater timing and began to communicate to those with the temperament to understand.

Ouspensky believed that, *"The building of cathedrals was part of a colossal and cleverly devised plan which permitted the existence of entirely free philosophical and psychological schools in the rude, absurd, cruel, superstitious, bigoted, and scholastic Middle Ages. — The Church was made an instrument for the preservation and propagation of the ideas of true Christianity, that is, of true religion or true knowledge which were absolutely foreign to it."* Visiting Paris in 1914 he had felt that, *"the real history of humanity, the history worth speaking of, is the history of the people who built Notre Dame."*

This intimation was triumphantly expressed in 1926 with the publication of *Le Mystere des Cathedrals* by an author known only as Fulcanelli. It caused an esoteric sensation the likes of which had not been seen since the furore surrounding the appearance of the Rosicrucian works in the early seventeenth century. Fulcanelli was an enigmatic figure whose true identity rapidly took on the form of a legend the modern form of which portrays him as a semi-immortal alchemist who occasionally manifests in spectacular circumstances. Regardless of such mythology, the book was obviously an arcane classic of the highest order.

Fulcanelli claimed that the cathedral of Notre Dame in Paris was a vastly complex book in stone. The statuary and its placement within the architectural scheme represent a Hermetic alchemical Qabalistic philosophy, an illuminated Gnostic inner Christianity. There had been hints of such ideas before but Fulcanelli's work definitively established such an ambience around the Gothic cathedrals. Chartres has become the main focus for such ideas in modern times. Fulcanelli's alchemical interpretation states that the first substance, the *prima materia* from which the universe was created, *"the very essence of things"*, is one and the same with *mater*. The cathedrals dedicated to the Virgin are alchemical temples demonstrating God's creation of life, *"the transformations of the original substance"* for, *"in the Ave Regina, the Virgin is properly called root (salve radix) to show that she is the principle and beginning of all things. 'Hail, root by which the Light has shone on the world.'"*

Solomon's Temple had been conceived of as the dwelling place of the Shekinah, the wisdom or bride of god. Bernard of Clairvaux's devotion to the Song of Songs, which extols that very principle, suggests interesting potential continuity with the cathedrals as temples of the Queen of Heaven, often likewise praised as a black and beautiful dazzling darkness. Even more intriguing is an architectural metaphysical theme that seems to link back to the western world's earliest religious structures. Hank Harrison in *The Cauldron and the Grail* compared megalithic Newgrange, where on a particular date a sunbeam enters into the building's womblike darkness, with Chartres whose architects famously engineered a similar phenomenon. It's well known that many Christian buildings were constructed on sites already sacred in earlier ages. How much did the movers and shakers of the Grail era know about their ancient predecessors? Why duplicate the light beam phenomenon? Harrison believes that the interiors of the cathedrals were deliberately womblike and were in effect a Grail that the Holy Spirit entered and fertilised. The megalithic temples had essentially the same purpose and a proto-Grail cult had existed from immemorial antiquity with its communion rites changing through history from skull cups to the likes of Suger's chalice.

Bernard of Clairvaux had presided over the pivotal Troyes synod that fully empowered the Templars. He was actually a nephew of Andre de Montbard, one of the original nine Templars. Graham Hancock has conjectured a possible trade-off of knowledge gained beneath Solomon's Temple for Bernard's patronage. It's a very short period of time from the 1128 synod to Bernard's involvement at Chartres. He had been assiduously cultivating a friendship with the Bishop there. When work on the tower began, he was present at the time, talking almost daily with the builders. Bernard had a definite interest in geometry, considering it to be god's major tool of creation. Coupled with his mystical Marian devotion, he seems a strong candidate for an intention to deliberately influence the new cathedral culture.

A large number of intriguing connections between significant game-players begin to be revealed. They become progressively more complex and the bigger picture of what was going on at the time increases in size at a dizzyingly exponential rate.

In 1128, the same year that the pope gave Holy Order status to the Templars, Hugh de Payens visited King Henry I in England. One of the other original nine founding members, Payen de Montdidier, became Grand Master of England. At his instigation a large building program was begun. A preceptory was built at Oxford on land given by Matilda, the daughter of the King and future mother of Henry II. It's clear that the moment the pope gave the nod, there were important people ready to help the Templars expand. At this time Geoffrey of Monmouth was a secular canon in Oxford and probably aware of a number of these developments. He may even have met Payen de Montdidier. Chretien de Troyes' *Perceval* was dedicated to Phillipe d'Alsace, Count of Flanders, crediting him as the source of the tale. Phillipe's father was a cousin of Payen de Montdidier. The area around Troyes was very much a Templar power base. Most of the original nine knights had been based in the general vicinity. The synod that confirmed their status as a Holy Order had been held at Troyes itself.

In *Parzival*, Wolfram Von Eschenbach tells how the Grail was guarded by *'Templeisen'*. This has often been taken as an obvious reference to the Templars. Galahad comes to a monastery in *Quest of the Holy Grail* where he receives a shield with the Templar design of the red cross on white background. It had once belonged to Joseph of Arimathea. These references may indicate inside knowledge or they may simply reflect the charisma of the Templars and a certain inevitability of tales concerning the miraculous and esoteric becoming associated with them.

SUFISM

In studying the European Middle Ages the most significant issue is the nature of the interaction between Christianity and Islam. It might seem at first that the crusades facilitated the main contacts between the two religions. The Templars are the usual suspects for any trafficking of esoterica. There were other areas of significant connection as well. Some contemporary analogies and parallels may serve to bring out the subtleties of the situation. Opposite systems can be economically dependent on each-other, ie the United States and the Soviet Union during the Cold War period. The West is the dominant cultural force in the world today. It exports all manner of things to developing countries as aid and exploitation, and in so doing exercises forms of control. Coca-Cola, McDonalds and Michael Jackson music can be found in some pretty obscure places. In a hundred years time they may be considered traditional there.

The CIA and KGB tried to be aware of political and religious groups, especially secretive ones propagating dissent, revolution or heresy. They liked to cultivate the option of manipulation and infiltration. Weapons might be sold to apparent opponents if it served the bigger picture. Wars came and went but were tolerated as long as an acceptable balance was kept and some sort of overall progress could be made.

That's how it's been in recent times. It's also how things were a thousand years ago when Christianity and Islam were the two power blocks. Aid and covert control were going out to undeveloped countries. Those countries were in Western Europe though. Islam was then *the* world civilisation. Their culture stretched from Spain to Indonesia, from Africa to China. Any history book would accept that we took a lot from the Arabs. Algebra and Arabic numerals in the realm of science. Arabic literary models and influences have been found in Dante, Chaucer, Shakespeare and Cervantes.

During the early Middle Ages, Spain could be said to have been the brain of the world. It was a meeting place of Arab, Jew, and Christian. The modern forms of the Qabalah, so crucial to the development of the western mystery tradition, came together there and found their way into Christian Europe. The Rabbinic school at Troyes would have felt the influence of the Spanish Qabalistic infusion. The city of Cordoba had 700 mosques, a palace with 400 rooms, and a city library with 400,000 books. Incredible ideas passed through. Mevlana Rumi, founder of the whirling dervishes, spoke of evolution. Ghazal discussed sex in a manner not unlike Freud. Ibn Al-'Arabi seemed to deal with Jungian archetypes. Hermetic literature also circulated. Spain was the most likely potential source of its dissemination into the Europe of the Grail epoch.

Western learning had been preserved in monasteries. Benedict established his order at Monte Cassino in 529, as the old forms of the Roman Empire dissolved. In 910, twelve monks from Monte Cassino founded the Abbey of Cluny. Within a century they had a thousand square miles of land under their control. A mission was sent to Spain where it was cordially received. They brought back algebra and logarithms. At Monte Cassino an Arab in residence translated scientific texts. The Cluniacs also greatly expanded the idea of pilgrimage. The Islamic Haj, the journey to Mecca, had proved its cultural value. It was Arabic glassmakers, heirs to a tradition steeped in alchemy who had been used to create the first stained glass windows in the west at St Denis.

It's fruitful to ponder on the state of affairs then. The crusades were at their peak. There was a huge propaganda in motion to smash Islam. War was occurring between the two cultures. Nonetheless, all of this exchange was able to continue. We may tend to think of those times as savage and intolerant but I wonder how Americans of the Macarthyite fifties would have felt about their top intellectuals and churchmen being involved in a constant exchange of information and ideas with the Soviet Union? Can we imagine Russians in residence at their top universities? I doubt it.

Something subtle may also have been communicated between the two cultures. According to Idries Shah's *The Sufis*, and Ernest Scott's *The People of the Secret*, all of the major esoteric mysteries of our European Middle Ages were either activated by the Sufis, the mystics of Islam, or contained a deliberate infusion of some kind by them. We're talking about the whole Hermetic package and alchemy, witchcraft, Rosicrucianism, the Qabalah, the tarot, court jesters, the Templars, the Order of the Garter, Freemasonry, the Troubadours, and Arthurian Grail literature. That's quite a list and it seems to be an outrageous claim.

Sufic schools are apparently not necessarily permanent like Christian organisations. They may fade in and out as the occasion demands. Being involved with them wouldn't inevitably mean leaving everyday life behind to live in some sort of monastery. Princes and bakers may equally be a part of it. Sufism is a nutrient for society. Its function is to be transmuted, not to leave unaltered traces. Their activities may be hard to spot without a certain preparation.

TROUBADOURS

The Hermetic and Templar aspects of the Arthurian mystery are controversial. Bringing in the Sufis may seem even more tenuous. Are there any cases of cultural transmission with a definite Sufi signature that clearly connect with Arthur and the Grail? The answer appears to be yes. And the Queen of England, the legendary Eleanor, is strongly involved. She had accompanied her first husband Louis VII of France on the Second Crusade. They had stopped at the crusader kingdom of Antioch, which was ruled by her uncle Raymond. All kinds of Christians and Moslems mixed together. Many crusaders were married to Saracen women. After becoming the Plantaganet Queen, she established a base for herself at Poiters. There she focused her attention on cultivating a Love Court of the Troubadours.

Each year in springtime, there was a period of mutually agreed truce when warfare between barons, princes, and kings ceased. During this time, the younger members of both French and English aristocracy would come together and mingle, imbibing all kinds of incredible ideas in a festival of culture presided over by Eleanor and her daughters. The more difficult her marriage to Henry became, the more time she gave to this remarkable phenomenon.

It's interesting to remember that when Eleanor was crowned Queen of France a chalice was used in the ceremony that was considered to actually be the one used in the last supper, in other words, most peoples idea of the Grail. She would hardly have been unaware of this. Nonetheless, the Grail literature that flourished around her did not affirm this. The implication is that the

Grail stories were clearly being used to promote ideas other than Christian mysticism.

The wandering hippie-like troubadour poets were often of aristocratic blood. Their movement had appeared, as if fully formed, virtually overnight. This is considered to be a characteristic element of Sufi operations. We even know who the first Troubadour was: Guillem, Duke of Aquitaine, Eleanor's grandfather. He'd been a crusader in the Middle East and also in Spain. His songs brought conflict with the church due to their sexual element. There's no question that the Troubadours had their roots amongst wandering Saracen mystic poets of Spain. One of the great experts on Arthurian literature, Roger Sherman Loomis, cites Ibn Hazm's *Dove's Neck Ring* as a textbook on Courtly Love. They sang for the love of a lady, mainly unobtainable, often married. Their material was so ambiguous it was difficult to know where one's sympathies were supposed to lie. The best example is the Arthur/Guenevere/Lancelot situation, their fundamental contribution to the mythos. Jean Markale believes that Eleanor, *"was used as a model for the Queen Guinevere of many of the Arthurian romances. The two women match each other in beauty and authority, in political awareness and amorous adventures. Both are surrounded by a conspiratorial atmosphere, both reigned for a long time."*

The Troubadours spread the idea of Courtly Love and chivalry, along with an idealisation of women, helping to reinject a missing female element into the culture of Christian Europe. Above all, they were vital in the dissemination of Arthurian literature. It may well be that something of the prestige of the Bard in Celtic Druidic culture lingered in their old lands, contributing something to the charisma of their Troubadour inheritors.

Chretien de Troyes was a courtier at Poitiers and a protege of Eleanor's daughter from her first marriage, Marie. In a work on Lancelot, he stated that it was she who had given him the controlling idea for the tale. Chretien's most famous work, the unfinished saga of Perceval, had introduced the Grail. That story had been supposedly given to him by Phillip of Flanders (remember his Templar link?), Marie's second husband. This was the matrix from which the cultural explosion began. All the major works, such as von Eschenbach's *Parzival,* follow within a few decades. After that, the material becomes overlaid with increasingly pious Christian interpolations. This again is supposedly a sign of a Sufi operation when a vast cultural form appears almost instantly, fully formed and perfect, and starts to decay within a generation when the goal has been achieved and the initiated impetus withdrawn.

Ouspensky said that, *"The culture of barbarism grows simultaneously with the culture of civilisation. But the important point is the fact that the two cannot develop on parallel lines indefinitely. The moment must inevitably arrive when the culture of barbarism arrests the development of civilisation and gradually, or possibly very swiftly, completely destroys it.*" At the peak of the Grail era, the forces of reaction and conservatism kicked back. Heresy was busted as never before. The Cathars became the victims of a prototype genocide. The rich culture of southern France that had nourished the troubadour love courts was devastated. The empire of Henry and Eleanor dissolved. Northern France came into the ascendant. The Templars were famously suppressed.

Perhaps some of the intuitive writers of the romances knew that the cultural climate that encouraged their creativity was a transient phenomenon. Some of them said that once the Grail quest had been completed, it and its initiates were withdrawn to some inaccessible realm. At first it travelled on the Templar ship with its red cross on white background sail, to Jerusalem. Eventually it travelled further still, to 'India'.

The twelfth century was one of the most extraordinary in the history of Europe. What a mixture! Christian, Celtic, Gnostic, Hermetic, and Sufi influences blending in extraordinary and rapidly shifting combinations. Light shining through stained glass windows. Light shining through the consciousness of a visionary nun enlivening her inner genius to give the world a gift of supernal music and creation spirituality. The stirring of the divine feminine. A baptism in cosmic consciousness, the divine krater being poured forth and more people willing and able to receive its blessings than ever before. A spectacular intimation of the potential dawning of an age of the Holy Spirit.

One symbol potentially unifies all this. The Grail. And what more civilising mission could be imagined than to envisage the ultimate heroism in the form of a quest to heal the earthly kingdom through the securing of the blessings of that vessel? What more inspiring and noble task did any creative artists ever aspire to? The Grail can serve as a doorway into an astounding expansive realm of true religious mystical consciousness. It has not arisen from the same influences that shape the history of crime, of barbarism. It represents the true well-spring of civilisation. The ever more insistent re-emergence of this archetype in the modern world warns and inspires us of the urgent necessity of re-connecting to the same levels of inspiration. I began to entertain a most disturbing idea: the twelfth century was in certain respects a more truly civilised time than the present day.

Glastonbury

THE ABBEY AND ARTHUR: POLITICS AND ESOTERICA

IN THE BACKGROUND of the emergence of the Plantaganet dynasty, the marriage of Henry and Eleanor, and the reigns of their two sons, are the crusades, the rise of the Templars, the building of the Gothic cathedrals, the developing cult of the Virgin Mary, and the full-blown appearance of the phenomenon of Arthur and the Grail. All of this is within a timescale of events crucial to the evolution of Glastonbury and the way it is perceived today.

When the Saxons arrived in Glastonbury they found a piously venerated small church, redolent of a mysterious antiquity. Rather than act as conquerors, they accepted what was in place and tried to create a functional unity with the resident Britons. Regardless of the obscure origins of the old church, the abbey developed in Saxon times into the most prestigious ecclesiastical establishment in the land, a burial place for saints and kings. In *King Arthur's Avalon* Geoffrey Ashe stated that, *"Here the Britons and Saxons first learned to live at peace and the vision of the United Kingdom was born."* The creation of England from Alfred's Wessex was simultaneous to Glastonbury's development as pre-eminent shrine of the Anglo Saxon kingdom. Even then, it was part of propaganda for a national mythos of sorts. No surviving evidence of that period however, mentions Arthur, Joseph of Arimathea, or the Grail.

It was obvious that the Norman conquerors would pay close attention to such an important part of the Saxon state. They certainly created an impact in Glastonbury. A new abbot was appointed. Thurstan seems to have been a bit of a mystic and began a typical Norman building programme but that's not what he's remembered for. He sought to impose a new style of liturgical chant. The monks resisted. It might seem a minor issue to modern eyes but appalling scenes ensued. Armed men came to enforce Thurstan's authority. Arrows were fired within the abbey buildings. Three monks were killed and eighteen wounded. The nationwide horror was such that King William withdrew Thurstan back to France. The conqueror's son later accepted a payment from the disgraced abbot to restore him to his position. He wasn't exactly welcomed back with rejoicing in the streets and died not long afterwards. A Saxon establishment had most definitely become a Norman one.

Henry I asked a nephew of his named Henry of Blois to become Abbot of Glastonbury Abbey, which he did in 1126 whilst still in his twenties. An ancestor of Henry known as Theobald the Cheat captured the area in France around Blois and the county of Chartres in the tenth century. From that time on the family was very much in the centre of some major early medieval esoteric action. The town of Blois is situated in the vicinity of Troyes. Henry had studied at Cluny at the very time it was attaining its greatest power and influence. He would have been well aware of developments at St Denis and in good communication with Chartres. Henry was considered to be an academic prodigy. The learning and philosophy behind the new style of architecture would have been part of the general mindset he brought to his new appointment at Glastonbury.

Henry also, with the special permission of the pope, uniquely took on the simultaneous role of Bishop of Winchester, then the main royal city in England. The royal mint was located there along with the great Domesday Book survey. He soon got down to serious business, initiating huge building programs, both ecclesiastical, at Glastonbury and Winchester, and secular, with a host of castles around the country. Glastonbury was soon transformed from a chaotic mess into the richest abbey in England. Many new buildings, including a bell tower, were constructed. The old church remained intact at that time and would surely have been given much attention by the new arrival. Henry would have been well prepared to appreciate any mysteries concerning its design and traditions.

Henry was a perfect example of the fact that churchmen were by no means separate from political activity. His father had been one of the earliest Templars, his mother a daughter of William the Conqueror. The usurper Stephen of Blois was his brother. There are hints that it was Henry himself who was the prime mover in the plot to bring him to power. He certainly played a major role in the civil war that followed. In one astonishing episode in 1141 he led an army besieging Matilda in Winchester itself. The city was torched and Matilda fled.

Geoffrey of Monmouth gives many mentions to Winchester. It's the beginning of it becoming an Arthurian location. Uther Pendragon was proclaimed King there. Arthur fights Mordred in the vicinity. There's no real precedent for a lot of his general championing of the city. Geoffrey was known to be concerned to advance his career. He is said to have composed his life of Merlin to please the Bishop of Lincoln. It could be that he wanted to get on the right side of the powerful Bishop of Winchester. Nor is it entirely unlikely that Henry could have made some suggestions to Geoffrey concerning his composition. Chretien de Troyes mentions Winchester in one of his Arthurian romances, *Cliges*, and seems to have a vivid knowledge of it. It's the first time the city is portrayed as where Arthur holds court. It has been suggested that Chretien may have visited Winchester in the retinue of Henry of Blois.

Henry was patron of William of Malmesbury. His historical work on Glastonbury Abbey, *De Antiquitate Glastonie Ecclesie*, appeared in 1129, within three years of Henry arriving, the same year he became Bishop of Winchester, within one year of the Templars becoming an official Holy Order, and before the appearance of Geoffrey of Monmouth. Its most famous passage strongly suggests the presence of some esoteric mystery within the old church. *"One can observe there upon the paving, in the forms of triangles and squares, stones carefully interlaced and sealed with lead. If I believe that some sacred mystery is concealed under them, I do no harm to religion."* The powerful royally connected abbot would surely have had some kind of control over what William published, so it seems likely he was happy to let that idea circulate, for whatever reasons.

The man who was Abbot of Glastonbury between 1126 and 1171 was the most powerful, important, and influential real historical character ever to have functioned there. A major political conspirator. A king maker. There can be little doubt that he was working with a significant agenda on many levels. He may well have influenced the two most important figures in the development of the Arthurian mythos, Geoffrey of Monmouth and Chretien de Troyes. He certainly oversaw the writing of a work on Glastonbury that contained information that's served as what Robert Bauval would call a 'Hermetic device', still drawing people into its mystery almost a millennia later.

Bernard of Clairvaux referred to Henry interestingly as a rival pope, old wizard of Winchester, and even whore of Winchester. Given Bernard's position in the Templar and Chartres stories, it is possible that he, and probably they, were already keeping an eye on events in Glastonbury before the Arthur's grave event brought it European fame. It may be that the Templars and Chartres schools were trying to establish a total esoteric initiatory network across Europe through the cathedral building programme and the cultural changes resulting from it. Chartres was built on the site of an old Druid centre and dedicated to the Virgin. Glastonbury had interesting similarities. Henry of Blois and William of Malmesbury were perhaps deliberately making a statement on behalf of the place suggesting that it was a pre-Templar repository of esoteric knowledge connected with architecture. Bernard of Clairveaux's pointed remarks about Henry may indicate the rivalries of different groups vying for influence, especially considering the

Blois family power base around the Chartres Troyes area.

When the old church, with its esoteric floor-plan, was destroyed by fire in 1184, the new Mary chapel was constructed, deliberately reproducing its original geometrical dimensions, which in turn appear to have served as the matrix for all subsequent extensions. The time of its rebuilding broadly coincides with the reconstruction of Chartres Cathedral, also following a disastrous fire, from 1194 to 1220. Few would now doubt that Chartres could be considered to be a book in stone. The official guide books accept the use of gematria in the proportions of the architecture, whereby the length between two features may embody through associations between numbers and letters some Biblical passage further expressed in statuary, and so on. The New Jerusalem of *Revelation* was a consistent inspiration for the decorative imagery of numerous ecclesiastical buildings of the Middle Ages. Considering that its geometry is so much a part of the biblical narrative, is it really likely that the cathedral builders, schooled in the seven liberal arts of which geometry was such an important element, would not have considered somehow utilising the design in their work? What are the chances that not the slightest nuance of such concerns was present in the newly emerging form of Glastonbury Abbey?

Henry II had helped to finance the reconstruction after the fire of 1184. A few years later, according to Gerald of Wales, he heard from *"an aged British singer"* specific details of Arthur's burial site in Glastonbury Abbey. The King himself passed this information to the monks. This does indicate his central role in what followed although he died before the results were uncovered.

A good case can be made for understanding the discovery as deliberate fraud for political propaganda. Henry II was in conflict with the Celts. Arthur had become a kind of messianic figure for the Welsh. His disappearance was a mystery. There was an ardent belief in his return. If his grave could be discovered such hopes would probably fade. Henry may also have recalled Henry of Blois' role in the usurping of his mother. He had driven her from Winchester with the city in flames. Not only that, Henry had been close to Thomas Beckett, funding him during a period of exile in France. It also seems there was contact between Henry of Blois and Eleanor during the time of her imprisonment by her husband. Establishing complete control on all levels, political and esoteric, over his former power base might have helped to lay some bad memories to rest and further confirm his supremacy for the sake of the dynasty he was conscious of founding.

In *The Divine King in England,* Margaret Murray speculated that the Anglo-Norman monarchs were a Frazerian cult. She saw giveaway signature signs in a number of early medieval events involving them. William Rufus was mysteriously killed in a hunting accident in the New Forest on the date of the old pagan feast of Lammas. Murray suggested that this might have been a sacrificial rite. Frazer believed that surrogate victims were sometimes chosen in place of the king when the ritual time cycles came round. Her wildest hypothesis was that the murder of Thomas Becket and Henry's subsequent scourging and repentance was just such an event. If Henry was part of a "king and the land are one" cult he wouldn't have wanted another divine king competing for the people's attention. Far better to establish Arthur as dead and himself as successor and embodiment of the tradition.

There are even stranger shadows in the background as well. Something happening in the dark of night. Remember the Wild Hunt? To the Norman aristocracy of Henry's time it wasn't looked on as a piece of archaic folklore but a disturbing contemporary reality. The *Anglo-Saxon Chronicle* of 1127 records, *"common gossip up and down the countryside that after February 6th many people both saw and heard a whole pack of huntsmen in full cry. They straddled black horses and black bucks while their hounds were pitch black with staring hideous eyes. This was seen in the very deer park of Peterborough town, and in all the wood stretching from that same spot as far as Stamford. All through the night monks who kept watch heard them sounding and winding their horns. Reliable witnesses who kept watch in the night declared that there might well have been twenty or even thirty of them".*

Gervase of Tilbury wrote that, *"the wood wardens... relate that on alternate days, about the hour of noon or in the first silence of night, by moonlight in the full of the moon they have very often seen a band of knights hunting and the noise of hounds and horns, who declared to those who asked that they were the fellowship and household of Arthur."* This account dates from 1190 and makes it clear that Arthur was the leader of the Wild Hunt.

Walter Map, writing in the twelfth century, mentions that such bizarre groups were widely manifesting during the reign of Henry II. They seemed to be involved in *"endless wandering, in an aimless round... and in them many persons who were known to have died were seen alive. They travel as we do, with wagons and sumpter horses, pack-saddles and panniers, hawks and hounds, and a concourse of men and women. Those who saw them first raised the whole country against them with horns and shouts... but they rose into the air and vanished suddenly."*

A Scooby Doo Mystery Inc investigation might uncover the actions of flesh and blood individuals engaged in some activity that benefited from having all potential witnesses too terrified and confused to intervene. Whatever was really happening, it was widespread, alien to the ruling class and potentially subversive of it. Display the body of its leader and you regain control. Maybe.

The earliest accounts of the Glastonbury excavation actually tell of the recovery of *three* skeletons. The anomalous addition was initially identified as Mordred. There was an immediate response of disbelief that Arthur's treacherous son would have been buried alongside him. The third skeleton rapidly disappeared, never to be mentioned again. This doesn't exactly boost the credibility of the event.

In *The Flaming Door*, Eleanor Merry wrote that, *"Whatever part the monks of Glastonbury or Henry himself are said to have played in this event is unimportant. What is important is that here is the sure touch of the hand of destiny; that here the curtain is finally rung down on the ancient mysteries of Britain – and of the world. For the word goes out that Arthur is dead."* According to this theory, a mystery tradition of immemorial antiquity finally vanished from the outer planes at that point.

There are other ways of looking at it. The male skeleton claimed to be Arthur was buried in a hollowed tree. Gerald of Wales suggests that Henry's Cymric informant had provided this very detail so perhaps it was then manufactured. It's a strange detail to use to try and increase the credibility of a medieval forgery though. A standard coffin would make more sense. Tree burial is an ancient custom known to the modern world through archaeology but unknown to twelfth century monks. The bones were those of a man of impressively large stature. It still doesn't mean that the body was Arthur's. It does lend credibility to the idea that the place was an isle of the dead where warriors may have been interred. The fact that the monks did find such an Arthur-like person is at least a little enigmatic. Remember the 1998 Cadbury 'boat' burial discovery pointing towards the Tor? If twelfth century monarchs and monks were trying to control Arthur, the genius loci intervened to affirm an Annwn/Avalon aspect of Glastonbury, ultimately making the myth stronger.

At the time of the discovery, Eleanor was actually governing England whilst her son Richard was away on crusade. On another level of the game, the efforts of the Queen and her daughter at the Love Courts were bearing fruit. They had been heavily involved in the cultivation and promotion of the Grail literature that was revitalising Celtic mythology by infusing it with all manner of esoterica in the context of Christian mysticism, thus ensuring that its motifs not only didn't die but entered into the greater culture, perhaps with more enduring power than ever before.

Eleanor had personal experience of the northern French Paris matrix and came to despise it. Bernard of Clairvaux was happy to see her divorced from the French king. He helped to arrange it. The Courtly Love culture was able to flourish because of the Plantaganet empires' need to assert a distinctive culture at odds with the northern French tales of Charlemagne and the austerity of Bernard of Clairvoux.

Whilst not necessarily suggesting a direct involvement of Eleanor with the Glastonbury event, there does seem to be a certain *something* just out of view behind the scenes subtly at work. Glastonbury can be profitably compared with the abbey of St Denis in Paris. Here too can be found a strange foundation legend involving an obscure Biblical character. Both sites were hallowed burial grounds for saints and kings whose history and sanctity could be used to boost the credibility of the contemporary royalty. Both places were vital in the dissemination of a national heroic mythos, whether of Arthur or Charlemagne. Both became the domain of remarkable royally connected mystical politicians in the form of Henry of Blois and Abbot Suger. Further figures of immense importance such as Eleanor and Bernard of Clairvoux occupy a shadowy zone that connects with both locations in different ways. Knights Templar walk between the camps as well.

Another glimpse of that *something* in the background of the 1190 event can be seen in the Earth Mysteries classic, *The Sun and the Serpent* by Hamish Miller and Paul Broadhurst, an account of a dowsing journey along the Michael ley line. The authors came to believe that earth energy of some kind does flow through its famous sites. Dowser Miller experienced it as two streams of what could be broadly called male-female force. They followed a sinuous path, weaving in and out between each other, occasionally meeting like the snakes of a caduceus wand. The points of their convergence were considered to be particularly powerful. One such place was the High Altar in Glastonbury Abbey. The nearby site where the bones of Arthur and Guenevere had been interred after their excavation in a black marble tomb seemed to be a strange island in the flow of the female current, which was dowsed as splitting and rejoining around it. The tomb of the royal couple also lies on a further alleged ley that runs right through the central axis of the Abbey, continuing on to Stonehenge. The authors felt that this simply couldn't be a random anomaly. Whoever selected the place for the tomb must have known about the flow of energy through the place. It was deliberate and served some arcane purpose. The whole configuration suggests an illustration in an alchemical manuscript.

From that moment Glastonbury became identified with the Isle of Avalon. This is yet another area of rancid disagreement. The discovery of the grave seemed to suggest some sort of logic: if Arthur was laid to rest at Avalon and he'd been found at Glastonbury then it must be Avalon. The Celtic traditions

of islands of the dead don't really suggest there was only one of them. The
name 'Avalon' may well have originally referred to a location other than
Glastonbury. What cannot be doubted is that all of the characteristics of
Avalon are present in Glastonbury. If it isn't the original one, it probably fits
the bill even better. We can perhaps recover the details of the place the name
derived from. Different theories have been propounded. A good case can be
made for Anglesey. Chances are that, unless one is a powerful clairvoyant,
such other locations may not feel like a living reality. The new Avalonians
would affirm that Glastonbury remains a *functional* Isle of Avalon to this
very day and, beyond the sneering of the debunkers, it is that which is of
most importance.

So began a golden age. The Arthurian mythos with its quest for the Grail
had inspired the whole of Europe. Glastonbury's fame as his resting place
gave it a unique status. The Abbey and its lands were almost an independent
state, having been granted unique privileges by successive monarchs. Abbots
sought to outdo each other with ever-larger building projects. Apart from old
St Paul's it became the longest church in England. The blessings of Our
Lady of Glastonbury seemed tangible.

PERLESVAUS

There is one other significant Grail romance of the time to place alongside
Chretien and Wolfram and there are a number of indications that it has a
strong Glastonbury connection to further expand the mystery. *Perlesvaus*
was written in an old form of French by an unknown author. Often known
as the *High History of the Holy Grail,* it takes up the story where Chretien
left off, and could be seen as another of the 'continuations'. A number of
characters and plot details refer back to the *Conte del Graal.*

It's stated that, *"the Latin from whence this History was drawn into
Romance, was taken in the Isle of Avalon, in a holy house of religion that
standeth at the head of the Moors Adventurous, there where King Arthur and
Queen Guenevere lie".* This is an obvious reference to Glastonbury Abbey
and is usually taken to infer that it must have been written following the grave
scenario. A landmark quite likely to be the Tor is described in the story,
suggesting that the author had definite local knowledge. Perceval is portrayed
as a descendent of Joseph of Arimathea. The man and the Grail are featured
in the text, but never linked specifically to Glastonbury.

Some critics believe *Perlesvaus* was written in the decade 1200-1210.
A date as late as 1250 has also been suggested. This means that it's difficult

to determine whether it comes before or after the work of Robert de Borron or the *Queste Del Saint Graal* and what its level of originality may be. Which work first mentions certain themes may perhaps only be of interest to scholars. An early copy was in the possession of the Lord of Cambrein in Flanders indicating the possibility that the author was from what was then Northern France.

Whoever did write it, and wherever they were based, they clearly had access to Celtic mythological material. *Perlesvaus* is permeated by it, perhaps more extensively than any other Grail romance, particularly featuring that most disturbing of motifs, the severed head. Despite that, it's also more militantly crusadingly Christian than the other works of the time. Resistors of the New Law of Christ are brutally killed.

Regardless of the issues over the dating of the text, there are a number of significant elements in the story that are unique. The 'Grail' changes form. It is clearly stated that it has five aspects, each manifesting amidst the usual light and fragrance. These are: 1) A crowned king crucified. 2) A child. 3) A man wearing a crown of thorns, bleeding from the forehead, palms, feet and side. 4) The fourth form is unspecified. 5) A chalice.

The Fisher King actually dies, a detail at odds with the standard version of the Grail story where his healing is of paramount importance. Perceval does put right his earlier failure at the Grail castle but not by asking the right question. He takes it by force of arms. Arthur and Guenevere have a son named Lohot. Their union is usually portrayed as childless. Lohot is murdered, and in another unique development, Guenevere subsequently dies of grief.

Alongside Perceval, Gawain and Lancelot feature as major characters of the quest. The three move through a recurring landscape of castles, chapels, forests, and meadows, meeting a bewildering sequence of maidens, hermits, knights, kings, deceitful dwarves and the occasional demonic giant.

A number of obvious themes and motifs recur throughout the story. The name Perlesvaus itself is explained as meaning essentially, 'Perceval the disinherited'. Rightfully held land is repeatedly stolen and heroically regained throughout the story by a number of characters. There are complex webs of family relationships and blood feuds. Instances of withheld and mistaken identity constantly move the plot along. The central character, Perceval himself, changes his shield and apparel, going unrecognised in the close company of members of his own family, such as his sister and uncle, the Fisher King, and knights he has previously met, Gawain and Lancelot. Perceval often mysteriously refrains from identifying himself in these situations. Characters ask the names of others and are sometimes refused the information. Quite why this is never gets explained.

There are a number of bizarre and grotesque set-pieces. When Perceval defeats the Lord of the Fens, who had stolen his mother's land, he has eleven of the Lord's men beheaded and their blood drained into a vat which their leader is then lowered head first into and left to drown. At one point two artificial men created by sorcery who wield giant hammers beat out the brains of nearly fifteen hundred people. In an ongoing vigorous round of combat, jousting with lances and swordplay on foot is portrayed in grim detail as armour is ripped and rendered, limbs and heads are hacked off, and horses collide and crash to the ground. Maidens, innocent and otherwise, are whipped, beaten, and killed as blood flows and piteous lamentations fill the air. The kind of person who likes to count how many times goats appear in the Bible and things like that might be gainfully employed totting up the number of severed heads featured. Here and there, an obliging hermit interpolates an interpretation for the benefit of the puzzled protagonists of the strange events they are experiencing. The explanations seem odd and unconvincing, usually hinging on the Old Law of the Jews and the New Law of Christ. The great Arthurian scholar Roger Sherman Loomis has stated, *"the author seems at times deranged,"* demonstrating *"savage vindictiveness"* and *"a taste for the gruesome."* Norma Lorre Goodrich went even further, referring to him as *"a psychopath like the filthy Marquis de Sade".*

The mysterious author's anonymity has been cited as an indication that he may have been a member of a military order. There are so many details given in the course of the story involving armour, weapons, and grisly descriptions of wounds that it seems possible he had been on a real battlefield. The Teutonic Knights are known to have encouraged anonymous poets in their order. Perhaps he was a Templar. They don't get a specific name-check but their presence in the story seems fairly clear. Perceval enters a castle containing thirty three initiates wearing white garments with red crosses. Their master claims to have seen the Grail.

A modern reader might also note that, although there are some fascinating snippets about the Grail, its five changes and so on, it doesn't really seem to be that important to the story. A lot of the other themes appear to be far more predominant.

One maverick critic has given considerable time and ingenuity to the enigma of *Perlesvaus*. Hank Harrison is probably best known as the father of rock and movie star Courtney Love. Father and daughter have had a bit of a tempestuous relationship to say the least. She accused him of feeding her LSD as a small child when he was manager of the Grateful Dead. He propounded the controversial theory that her famous husband Kurt Cobain died not through suicide but murder. Far more interesting to me is Harrison's decades long interest in the Grail and all matters pertaining thereto. He studied at the Warburg Institute with the legendary Frances Yates. It was his major published work, *The Cauldron and the Grail,* that postulated continuity from megalithic times to the Gothic cathedral builders via such themes as the light beam orientation through the long barrows and cathedrals into the primal womb of the Goddess, with the mystery served from vessels that evolved from skull cups to Grail chalices.

Harrison has also produced a number of essays which centre around *Perlesvaus,* the mystery of its authorship and the nature of its meaning. Their content is contentious and provocative, unlikely to convince academics. Although I am far from comfortable with a lot of his details, once again I get the feeling of that *something* that does lead into the true temple of the mysteries being conveyed. One statement by him is worth remembering whilst entering into the contentious historical material he has assembled. *"The Grail is not an object, but rather an initiation, a ceremony, which transforms the supplicant from simple soul to brilliant mind."*

From Chretien onwards, the early romance authors used what is generally considered to be a kind of literary convention, claiming to refer to source material of some kind, a mysterious lost book of the Grail. With the story of Arthur's grave being so famous, it may be that Glastonbury was invoked in the way that Geoffrey of Monmouth talked of ancient documents or Wolfram talked of Spain. They could be stylistic devices to gain credibility. There might be no truth in the assertions at all. Harrison contends that such a work really existed and was in fact the *Perlesvaus.* He goes further still by contending that it was written by Henry of Blois who in turn was making use of an even earlier text.

His chain of associations begins in Tudor times, just after the tragic end of Glastonbury Abbey. A chronicler named Bales mentioned a "First Book of the Holy Grail" written by a hermit bard astronomer historian. This evokes the kind of figure who was on the cusp of the transition from Druidism into so-called Celtic Christianity. The work was allegedly famous in the time of King Ine, the Saxon who bestowed lavish grants upon the Abbey and funded building there. Harrison suggests Gildas as a possible author. The obvious problem is that Bales is a late source and the absence of any version of the material over the previous thousand years can be brought against it. It is nonetheless intriguing that the Helinandus fragment concerning the monk's vision and subsequent production of a Grail book was dated at 717, a period within the reign of King Ine.

Why would Harrison think of Gildas as a possible writer of a lost source book of the Grail? The saint is best known for his work *Concerning the Ruin and Conquest of Britain*. He lived during the Arthurian period and is often brought into academic controversies because, as we have seen, he discussed the battle most famously associated with the warlord without mentioning his name. British traditions depict him as a scholar hermit who is linked with Glastonbury Abbey and finally buried there. It is known that he spent time in Brittany where another strand of tradition was established around him.

Harrison makes much of a painting discovered in underground chambers at Chartres Cathedral in 1972. It allegedly depicts Gildas giving Mass to Nicodemus and Joseph of Arimathea. This is a very early depiction of the fabled Glastonbury founder. If Gildas is serving them this implies some strange seniority even though their lives preceded his by centuries. Harrison speculates that he may have been part of an alternative apostolic succession, the line of transmission that the genealogies tracing the Grail knights back though the Fisher Kings to Joseph try to establish. This extraordinary artwork was apparently, *"ruined by a bad attempt at reconstruction and certain items are now erased from it, most notably the golden chalice."* Harrison claims to have photos of the original form of the picture.

In this version of events we have Gildas as a link between Glastonbury and Chartres. The Grail source book is somewhere in the background of early events at both these major locations. Henry of Blois would have been aware of and had access to it. William of Malmesbury refers to his patron as a great writer, *"remarkable, besides his splendid birth, for his literary skills"*. Nothing seems to survive of any of this work. Harrison believes otherwise. He asserts that the basic form of *Perlesvaus*, whatever later adjustments were made to it, was written either by, or under the direction of Henry, probably using the earlier Gildas work for inspiration.

Chretien was an established literary figure but he did seem to quantum leap with his Grail tale. In 1170 Eleanor had returned to France, setting up court at Poitiers. It seems she had contact with Henry of Blois during the time of her English imprisonment. Considering her cultural interests, she would have probably travelled with books and manuscripts. Harrison contends that Eleanor may well have made available to her daughter Marie, Chretien's patron, material that had belonged to her great uncle Henry of Blois. Such items could have contained esoteric material and general Glastonbury lore. This may have included the legendary Grail source book.

In one of the continuations of Chretien, authorship of the original Grail book from which the tale was derived was ascribed to a Master Blihis, sometimes rendered as Blaise. Harrison suggests that this is a phonetic variant of Blois caused by regional accent pronunciations.

Harrison portrays *Perlesvaus* as a multi-levelled initiatory document, as esoterically loaded as Wolfram's *Parzival*. It contains material that reaches back through Celtic Druid times to the megalithic era. It also includes connections with the earliest years of Christianity and its links with the Qumran community, the generators of the Dead Sea Scrolls. Something of this was present in the background behind the rise of the Templars and the Gothic cathedral epoch. Harrison postulates the existence of some sort of cult of which Blois was connected that was behind the First Crusade and had deliberately set out to recover obscure relics and knowledge of the early days of Christianity. There are strands of mystery cult Hermeticism as well.

A major theme of the story concerns Perceval's mother, who is referred to as the Widowed Lady. Her lands and castles had been taken by hostile forces. As well as the associations modern readers would note regarding her designation and Freemasonry, Harrison feels that the Widowed Lady carries nuances of the Goddess, the Celtic Church, the Cathars and other heretics whose land had been seized by the pope. Henry of Blois' own mother was widowed when he was a baby. Despite being a daughter of William the Conqueror she had to do a deal with the Vatican whereby she set up convents for nuns in order to ensure her own survival. In functional terms, she had lost her lands. The theme may have also have hinted at the Henry II/Eleanor conflict.

The story of *Perlesvaus* really gets going with some adventures of Gawain, who Harrison sees as *"a young Templar initiate on a pilgrimage through prehistory and that he represents the hopes of more than one alternative religious faction."* His character embodies some very archaic strata. His famous encounter in another tale with the Green Knight connects back to the kind of shamanism of the hunt seen painted on cave walls. *"I see, in Gawain, Lancelot and Perceval, different faces of the old tricephalic god (Hermes Trismegistus). The trefoil spiral at Newgrange, date 3100 BC represents the same idea."*

Gawain is set a task before he can enter the Fisher King's castle and see the Grail. He has to recover the sword that beheaded John the Baptist from a pagan king. It seems that the sword presented to Perceval at the start of the Grail feast in Chretien's tale is being deliberately identified as the beheader of the Baptist. The entire story is stated to have begun on the midsummer feast of John so searchers for Johannite heresies have a few details to entertain themselves with.

In the Grail castle, the usual procession appears and a feast begins. Gawain has three sightings of the Grail. The first occurs when two damsels appear with the cup and lance, which is allowed to bleed into it. *"Gawain gazes at the Grail and it seems to him that there is a chalice within it, albeit there was none at the time."* The next time he, *"seemed to behold in the midst of the Grail the form of a child"*. In the final appearance, Gawain sees the crucified Christ, pierced by a spear. These transformations may echo the qualities of Celtic regenerative cauldrons. Despite having begun his quest in full knowledge of Perceval's earlier failure and being repeatedly prompted by his fellow diners, Gawain is so awe-struck by these visions that he neglects to ask the right questions. The scene has many similarities to Chretien's depiction but also some interesting differences. The Fisher King is absent from the hall during the feast. Angels rather than squires bear the candelabra. The Grail hovers in the air at one point. There are twelve knights present, who are all over a hundred years old, although they don't look it.

Harrison believes that the Fisher King has been deliberately portrayed in *Perlesvaus* with features suggestive of both the Templar and Cathar initiates.

"The Fisher King is Hermes guarding the Krater Hermetis, the God of light guarding the inner chamber, the priest of Eleusis guarding the womb of the Great Goddess." Ultimately, *"the Fisher King is the final composite of the tricephalic hero fulfilled, aged and seeking an heir"*. *"Perhaps part of the Grail vision is the realisation that one must eventually take over the job of the Fisher King. This is a great responsibility, without question identical to the Masonic tradition wherein the master of the temple retires and selects a successor."*

After Gawain's failure, the quest is taken up by Lancelot and finally, Perceval. The Grail Castle actually gets captured by the bad guys but Perceval single-handedly sorts out this little problem barely half way through the story. Before he does so, there is an enigmatic brief moment when his presence is sufficient to ensure the long prophesied opening of a tomb that turns out to contain his ancestor Joseph of Arimathea. Not a lot is made of this potentially momentous event. With the Grail castle secure and Perceval's family honour upheld, a second narrative dynamic leads up to a finale where he finally takes on a major villain, the Black Hermit, who is in fact none other than Lucifer, the Lord of Hell. It has been suggested that the action deliberately models the *Book of Revelation*. The overcoming of the Black Hermit seems very brief and underplayed for the dramatic climax of the book. Perceval unhorses and wounds him. He is not actually killed. His followers seize him, uncover a huge pit and fling him in. This happens to Satan in *Revelation*.

Is it feasible that Henry of Blois could have written this text? A lot of the general ambience suggests the time after his death when Jerusalem had been lost to Saladin. It was perceived as a calamitous event indicative of the

Last Days of *Revelation* having arrived and provoked an intense crusading zeal exemplified by Richard the Lion Heart. The cultural spiritual mood of the time was considerably different from when the holy city was in the possession of the crusaders a few decades earlier. The feeling in *Perlesvaus*, with its intense violent advocacy of the New Law of Christ, seems to reflect this.

What we know of Henry suggests a man of some considerable culture and refinement. He did strongly involve himself in politics and played a part in the destructive civil war but is the repeated brutal graphic violence of *Perlesvaus* really his style? I don't feel it is. If Henry was responsible in some way for the majority of the text, another additional later level of material would need to have been interpolated.

JOSEPH OF ARIMATHEA

In 1189, the same year that Henry II died, a cousin of his became abbot of Glastonbury. Henry de Sully had been abbot of Fecamps abbey in France. It's rather interesting that the place claimed to possess a sample of the blood of Christ and had become a major pilgrim site as a result. The new abbot was a worldly man. He was in charge when the grave was uncovered. It doesn't seem out of the question that he may have played some part in the promotion of Arthur and the one additional element in the Glastonbury mythos that remained to be added.

It's shortly after this time that Joseph of Arimathea finally appears and it's in an immediately contentious context. There are certain problems with William of Malmesbury's history of the abbey. The earliest surviving copy dates to about 1247, over a century after it was originally written. Scholars can easily determine that the Glastonbury scribe who produced it has made some significant additions to the text. The now familiar Joseph story first surfaces there. We have the gift of twelve hides of land to the saint and his party and the dedication of the Old Church to the Virgin Mary. It does seem clear that it is a response to both Robert de Borron's work and Arthur's grave. That doesn't definitively mean that the story has no historical truth to it but it does show how the form and flavour of the enduring mythos had been strongly shaped by the larger events of the Grail era. At this point the fundamental aspects of the Glastonbury legends have finally assembled together for Joseph is already linked to the Grail. The combination of Joseph, Grail, Arthur and Glastonbury was ready for development. Sceptics can, of course, refute it all as typical examples of an institution seeking to validate itself through the creation of an illustrious legendary pedigree, a standard medieval procedure.

About a century later, the story had become fully assimilated into the Glastonbury medieval blend. John of Glastonbury had produced *Cronica sive Antiquitates Glastonienses Ecclesie* around 1342. He recorded words attributed to Melkin, a Dark Age Welsh bard, believed in the late Middle Ages to have been a real historical figure. Geoffrey of Monmouth's Merlin prophecies had been hugely successful. Melkin may have been an attempt to cash in on the formula.

"The Isle of Avalon, greedy in the burial of pagans, above others in the world, decorated at the burial place of all of them with vaticinatory little spheres of prophecy, and in future it will be adorned with those who praise the Most High. Abbadare, powerful in Saphat, most noble of pagans, took his sleep there with 104,000. Amongst them Joseph de Mamore, named 'of Arimathea', took everlasting sleep. And he lies on a forked line close to the southern corner of the chapel with prepared wattle above the powerful venerable Maiden, the thirteen aforesaid sphered things occupying the place. For Joseph has with him in the tomb two white and silver vessels filled with the blood and sweat of the prophet Jesus. When his tomb is found, it will be seen whole and undefiled in the future, and will be open to all the earth. From then on, neither water nor heavenly dew will be able to be lacking for those who inhabit the most noble island. For a long time before the Day of Judgement in Josaphat will these things be open and declared to the living. Thus far Melkin."

A tremendous amount of ingenuity has been expended in attempting to understand this bizarre material. Words and phrases get juggled around and slightly altered. The above translation/version comes from notable Glastonbury scholar James Carley. A few things about the passage seem fairly clear. It is accepted that John had access to a version of *Perlesvaus*. The story included a scene where a sarcophagus tomb of Joseph of Arimathea was discovered and opened. The Melkin passage identifies Glastonbury as a major pagan burial site. Joseph seems to be categorised *'Amongst them'*. The reference to *'the prophet Jesus'* seems highly likely to be Muslim influenced. It simply isn't Christian parlance. Other items are more open to conjecture. The *'spheres of prophecy'* are often taken to indicate a possible zodiac design on the floor of the Abbey that may be what William of Malmesbury was referring to. Others favour crystal scrying balls. The *'forked line'* has been interpreted as a geometric pointer to the location of Joseph's tomb. There may be a hint of alchemy in *'heavenly dew'*. The vessels containing blood and sweat are normally rendered in English as 'cruets'. This is not a standard Grail image and has an alchemical nuance as well.

There is also a strong indication that the Abbey cemetery was one with a widespread legendary reputation for sanctity. Elsewhere in John of Glastonbury an account is given of the crusading adventures of Rainald of Marksbury who was captured by a Sultan and released only after he had obtained for his captor some earth from Glastonbury's cemetery. The sultan discusses Joseph with the crusader. This tale may well have influenced the form of the Melkin material. Assuming there is any accuracy in the story, it is intriguing to think of an Islamic Sultan believing in some special sacredness associated with Glastonbury.

In the time of the flourishing of the romances, and shortly before the full emergence of the Joseph Glastonbury mythology, there were other strata of mysterious material circulating about him. In *Twenty-First Century Grail*, Andrew Collins discovered that these may also have been a factor in the Melkin prophecy. The *Flores Historiarum* of Roger of Wendover, published in 1228, records an extraordinary tale. An Armenian bishop was visiting the Cathedral and Abbey Church of St Alban where the monks asked him if he knew anything of Joseph of Arimathea. This in itself shows that he was a subject of interest at that time. The reply was astonishing. Yes, he knew all about Joseph because he had met and dined with him! He was now called Cartaphilus. We have here perhaps the earliest written record of what became the medieval legend of the Wandering Jew. There are a number of variants but the basic theme is of a figure who had witnessed the crucifixion, usually mocking Christ in some way, and was told by Jesus that he will see his return. This confers a kind of immortality upon him. He goes on a marathon walkabout, needing to rest for a kind of Dr Who regeneration every hundred years or so.

The great thing about the Wandering Jew was that he would turn up unannounced for lunch over periods of hundreds of years. Assorted confused and generally gobsmacked people have given accounts of mysterious encounters. Nutters have assuredly been drawn towards the archetype and curiously possessed by it. No doubt the occasional romantic mystic with a liking for drama has felt the need to impersonate the wanderer. It's an audacious free-lunch blag. Witnesses have probably allowed credulity and lack of critical intelligence to distort their memories. The myth is nonetheless a strangely compelling one. There are images in common with legends of alchemical immortality. How did Joseph get mixed up here? He was certainly a fabled wanderer. Is that all there is to it? What actually really happened to the Armenian bishop?

John of Glastonbury represents the final coming together of the full form of the Joseph mythos. As well as the Melkin passage, a family tree linking

Joseph through to Arthur is included which seems obviously influenced by *Perlesvaus*. Modern commentators who get irritated with Grail seekers often declare that the romances were always considered to be fiction and any attempt to read truth into them is futile. In Glastonbury at least, on two occasions, with the interpolation in William of Malmesbury's text, and with John, Grail romances are treated as sufficiently authoritative in some sense as to provide credibility for accounts intended to be considered as historical. This at least shows a different mindset at work then.

If Glastonbury was the famous school of forgery that its denigrators contend and the monks were not averse to manufacturing a celebrity grave then much could surely be gained from producing the Arimathean. Like Arthur they would have in their favour the fact that nobody else had already laid claim to such a relic. What actually did happen is unclear and confusing.

It may be that John's work had been stimulated by a visit from Edward III to Glastonbury in 1331. The monarch and his queen had paid lavish public respects to Arthur and Guenevere's tomb. It was a major validation of Glastonbury's status and mythology. Edward had a definite interest in such matters and this was a factor in his later foundation of the Order of the Knights of the Garter.

In 1345, royal permission was granted to a John Blome of London to search for Joseph of Arimathea's body in the grounds of Glastonbury Abbey. An anonymous East Anglian chronicler later stated that the tomb had been found in 1367. If this was the case then there would have been no need to mount a further excavation in 1419. A number of bodies were unearthed and it appears that one was tentatively identified as the saint. By 1424 an English representative at the church Council of Sienna clearly stated that Joseph had indeed been found. It might be expected that such an event would be the sensation of the Christian world and generate volumes of controversy. It all seems to fade from view until a little later the claims are being played down.

The penultimate abbot of Glastonbury, Richard Beere, developed a full-blown cult of Joseph, creating a crypt chapel for him where a statue oversaw miraculous healings. This was directly beneath the Mary Chapel. In the years of ruination, one collapsed in to the other. The floor of today's chapel is in fact the level of the Joseph crypt. The creation of it involved what would today be considered an archaeological catastrophe as evidence of the sites earlier history was removed through the downward digging. One would expect the remains of the saint, if such items were claimed to exist, to have been very much at the forefront of his crypt chapel cult scene. It all seems dimly lit now. Divergent versions remain to tantalise us.

After the dissolution a former monk named William Good stated that although Joseph was buried somewhere in Somerset, nobody knew exactly where. It may have been in the Abbey grounds but a strange tradition also linked him to Montacute. Maybe Good was protecting the secret. It wasn't the best of times for relics, statues, and the tombs of saints. There are other accounts of a tomb in the crypt chapel. Modern Glastonbury folklore, as collated by the major champion of Joseph, the Rev Lionel Smithett Lewis, tells of the sarcophagus remaining in place until 1662, when it was stealthily moved by night into St John's churchyard. It fell off the radar of awareness until 1928 when Lewis transferred it to inside the church where it remains in the present day. The tomb does seem to be late fifteenth century and of a size suggestive of a high status internment. Lewis claimed that it bore signs of having been moved. Known as the John Allen tomb due to the letters JA allegedly inscribed upon it, no attempt at all in the present day is made to associate it with Joseph. Indeed it is covered with a cloth. The excellent stained glass window depiction of Joseph nearby attracts far more attention. Lewis wrote a still popular work on Joseph but he is generally considered to be a virtual crank and his handling of source material has not impressed scholars.

Any burial site of Joseph of Arimathea would obviously be considered to be a unique place. His original tomb was the location for the fundamental event of the Christian religion. Whilst in there, Jesus went down to hell and back, resurrecting from the dead. Some have detected hints of a mystery cult in the Gospel tales. Jesus and Lazarus may have been involved in an initiatory rite. Perhaps likewise Jesus and Joseph. If so, that makes the Arimathean a major figure, as the overseer of the supreme initiation of Jesus. This helps confer a unique status on the role of Joseph and perhaps suggests that his final resting place would be one of particular sanctity.

There's more than a hint of magic and alchemy about the artefacts associated with his Glastonbury jaunt. The flowering staff has many possible levels of meaning, including that of a geometer's measuring rod, but is indubitably first and foremost, a wand. The chalice and cruets suggest the virtues of the philosophers' stone, the process of transmutation. The figure of Joseph that emerged during the Middle Ages has more than a hint of the Hermetic magus about him. He seems to be lying in his tomb like Christian Rosenkreutz.

The Joseph story has left us with perhaps the last functioning medieval-type saintly relic. Supposedly he arrived at Wearyall Hill and planted his staff into the ground. It sprouted and became the famous Holy Thorn. The current form of the story doesn't appear during the days of the Abbey but the thorn is of a type originating in the Middle East. Perhaps a Crusader brought it. Geoffrey Ashe delights in affirming how the enigma of Glastonbury often manages to supply such typically annoying little details to irritate the sceptic. Alongside Arthur, arguments about the historicity of the Joseph Glastonbury connection probably have centuries left to run. What's important for me is the sense of seeing through the story another glimpse of that *something*. The Arimathean mythos has impacted significantly on the greater life of the nation. An extreme form of the tale has Joseph as the uncle of Jesus. He comes to Britain with the young Christ as part of an involvement in the Cornish tin trade. It appears to be this idea that inspired William Blake to write the words that, now known as *Jerusalem*, have since been set to music and become our 'second national anthem.'

> *"And did those feet in ancient time*
> *Walk upon England's mountains green?"*

I'm not quite sure if the sceptical academics and general haters of Glastonbury would like to remove all such manifestations from our culture. I would refer them to the works of Jung, Joseph Campbell, and Mircea Eliade concerning myth as a vital natural human function, necessary to the health and sanity of the individual and body-politic, and a measure of the well-being of the society in which it arises.

MEDIEVAL CRYSTAL CONSCIOUSNESS

There is one mystery of medieval Glastonbury that perhaps makes more tangible the subtle influences that seem to reach from Abbot Suger and St Denis. It is explored in *The Ancient Secret* by Flavia Anderson, a work of remarkable originality in the correlation of unusual historical data. Anderson supports the hypothesis of Jessie Weston that behind the Grail literature lay some kind of heretical ceremonial, a cult linking pre-Christian times to the era of the Knights Templar. The evidence she puts forward is complex and detailed. Sufficient to say here that it deals with the use of light and crystal in religious rituals, particularly during the Christian Middle Ages.

In the medieval romances, perhaps the most consistent manifestation of the Grail presence is blinding light. Anderson believes that this was not just a spiritual metaphor but a real record of a tangible phenomenon. She enters into an extensive consideration of sacred and perpetual fires of antiquity. They were often lit using concave mirrors and crystals to focus the sun's rays. It was considered a marvel that a stone that could ignite fire would stay cold and unburned. Interestingly enough for New Agers and cynics who might think crystal healing is a recent invention, they were associated with medical treatment. An Orphic poem recommends placing a crystal that has just been used to kindle fire against the kidneys for relief of pain. These mirrors and crystals were special cult objects, guarded by an elite in temples.

Anderson wonders if the silver platter of the Grail procession and Wolfram's stone may have been such artefacts. There certainly seems to be a fire association with the stone that *"by its magic the wondrous bird The Phoenix, becometh ashes, and yet doth such virtue flow from the stone, that afresh it riseth renewed from the ashes' glow."* Clearly, the Grail stone produces fire. There's a bizarre scene in *Parzival* where the Fisher King figure's wound periodically causes more pain and he is given relief by having a spear thrust into it. Anderson believes the spear is a shaft of sunlight and finds a reference by the classical author Pliny of the use of crystal fire for cauterising wounds. Is this what's being depicted?

The ritual crystals would need to be framed in some kind of setting that would more than likely have an ornamental quality. They would require a handle, in order to be held up to catch the sun's rays. Anderson ranges far and wide in examining possible examples. She looks at the motif of the tree, as wood manifests fire. A crystal set in a stylised tree seems to be depicted on Babylonian seals, Norse legends, and Jewish temple artefacts. The Qabalah talks of a special state of knowledge given to Moses as the 'Luminous Mirror of the Tree of Life.' Galahad makes a tree of gold and precious stones around the Grail in the *Queste del Saint Graal* and it may be just such an object that's being referred to.

What of that other Hallow, the sword? Once the sacred fires had been lit they are used to kindle other fires. *The Golden Bough* and the works of Mircea Eliade are full of this kind of thing. During New Year renewals in various cultures, all fires might be extinguished. A single fire at the sacred centre would then regenerate the whole world. The means of this was a fire-brand, borne in Bronze Age male cultures by a king. It happened in Druidic Ireland, at Tara. Anyone lighting a fire before the king did could be killed. The new fire would be kept burning. The king and the fire were strongly linked. He might have a special torch that was kept burning separately from the communal fires. In a Ugandan example, if he died, it would be extinguished and an announcement made that "the fire has gone out." Flaming torches from these ritual fires might accompany an army into battle.

The most famous of all swords, Arthur's Excalibur, is often referred to as the *'brand.'* Anderson believes it is strongly linked to the fire-brand royal cultus. When Arthur dies, the sword is thrown into water. What about when he received it from the Lady of the Lake? A powerful means of kindling fire is through a hollow glass sphere filled with water. It focuses sunlight very effectively. Fire from water. A holy mystery to the ancients.

What's all this got to do with Glastonbury? There is an extant seal used by John Chinnock, one of the later abbots. On one side it features images of three female saints. In the middle is the Virgin Mary, holding the infant Jesus and some lilies. The modern day Catholic Church of Our Lady of Glastonbury used this image as the model for a beautiful statue that graces their shrine. Her companions on the seal are St Margaret of Antioch, seen standing over a dragon, and St Catherine of Alexandria who is holding her famous wheel. Around the edge are some words in Latin: *"Testis Adest Isti Scripta Matrix Pia XPI Glastonia."* *"There is at Glaston, as witness to this writing, the Holy Matrix of God."* Anderson entered into a prolonged examination of those words, involving correspondence with the British Museum. The seal is slightly damaged. There has always been an assumption that *'Holy Mother of God'* is being referred to. The word appears to be *'Matrix'* rather than *'Genetrix'* which is the usual term for the Virgin Mary. Matrix is a strange term to use. It tends to mean mould, cavity or cup, or the ore or rock in which a jewel may be embedded. Anderson believes it refers to *a* Grail object of some kind venerated at Glastonbury.

The Virgin's companions are an intriguing choice. Both are deemed by Catholic scholars to have probably never existed and were eventually removed from the calendar of saint's days. St Margaret of Antioch has a colourful biography. She was a sickly child and was raised by a nurse in comparative solitude. Nonetheless, she was spotted by the Governor of Antioch who got the hots for her. She resisted in archetypal virtuous manner and got slung into a dungeon with a serpent-dragon. Despite holding up a cross to defend herself, the monster swallowed her whole. The power of the cross then kicked in and the monster was split wide open and Margaret escaped, helped by our very own St George. Her name is generally taken to mean 'Pearl'. St George's spear is taken by Anderson to mean a shaft of sunlight and Margaret the Pearl, is the vessel it shines through.

St Catherine is always associated with the flaming wheel of her martyrdom. She was supposedly a Pharaoh's daughter and a Platonic philosopher who converted to Christianity. A wicked Emperor tried to win her back to paganism. She refused. He had her bound on a spiked wheel that when set in motion would rend her flesh. An angel brought down fire from heaven, destroying the monstrous contrivance. Catherine was beheaded instead. Anderson gives examples of the sun symbolised by a wheel and suggests that cult crystals may sometimes have been kept in the hub of a special wheel.

She believes that Catherine herself was actually such a crystal and the wheel was the fire focused through it.

Mary is shown holding the infant Jesus with one hand and lilies in the other. Fleur-de-Lys was originally spelt *'Fleur-de-Luce'* meaning 'Flower of Light.' Artistic depictions of the Annunciation, where Archangel Gabriel brings the news of her miraculous conception, usually show her accompanied by lilies. Over the centuries many Christians have puzzled over the Virgin Birth. In trying to understand how such a thing could be possible, one metaphor became predominant. Light can shine through glass, leaving it physically unchanged. *"Any 'vessel' which could thus receive the sun's rays and beget the fire-child without the intervention of an earthly male element was thought of as a 'virgin' vessel."* It takes on some quality of the divine feminine, the Earth Goddess in antiquity and the Virgin Mary in Christian times.

There is a strange story found in the Grail romances, *Prose Perceval* and *Y Seint Greal*. Arthur's squire visits a chapel where a dead knight is laid out by the altar. The Virgin Mary and the Devil are vying for his soul. The squire seizes the opportunity to steal a candlestick. The theft is spotted and the scurvy knave fatally wounded in the thigh. Arthur goes to investigate the chapel and finds a hermit saying Mass. The Virgin appears. A flame brighter than the sun then comes through the window and descends upon the altar.

Perlesvaus features a version of the tale. John of Glastonbury possibly had access to a unique form of that text that in turn inspired him to locate the chapel at Beckery, on the outskirts of Glastonbury, a place associated with Brigit. The door is guarded by two hands holding flaming swords. After the saying of Mass, instead of the manifestation of flame, the Virgin Mary gives Arthur a crystal cross. It was this miracle that established Arthur's Marian devotion and the subsequent embellishing of his shield with her image. John states that the cross was given to the Abbey and still existed in his day, the fourteenth century. There were times in the year when it was carried in procession.

Anderson believes that the cross would have had a Grail stone crystal set in its centre. It would have been used to bring down fire from heaven, through focused sun light. The use of three figures on the Abbey seal that all have similar associations is taken to be a deliberate representation of such mysteries. The artefact doesn't feature in later abbey inventories and may therefore still be hidden somewhere in situ. Amongst many relics claimed by the medieval monks of Glastonbury Abbey was the very vase of lilies that the Virgin was holding when the angel appeared.

In these motifs continuity can be discerned that connects back to Abbot Suger and St Denis. Alongside the spectacular chalice was another considerable treasure. A lenticular crystal carved with an intricate depiction of the crucifixion would surely have been part of the divine light extravaganza there. It used to hang above the altar. At least two Glastonbury abbots, Henry of Blois and Henry Sully had sufficient French connections to have been aware of such things and perhaps set up a Glastonbury version. Sully seems a good bet as the Fecamps blood of Christ relic legend has a distinctly peculiar form. After being scraped from the body after the crucifixion, some blood hardened into a small crystal ball that was later placed in a tree that ended up inside a pillar in the abbey. Anderson considers this imagery to be indicative of the presence of her main themes.

DISSOLUTION AND REBIRTH

Very soon after the triumphant emergence of the Mary chapel from the ashes of the great conflagration and the eternal anchoring of Arthur at Avalon, Glastonbury Abbey became a pawn in political games played by worldly churchmen vying for power and influence. During the reign of John ugly scenes twice occurred with armed men arriving to brutalise the monks, inflicting torture, imprisonment, banishment, and even death. It was an intimation of things to come. Although Glastonbury was spared the fate of the Cathars and Templars in the short term and went on to keep the dream alive for abundant centuries ahead, the final denouement was appalling.

In November 1539 onetime Renaissance *wunderkind* Henry VIII perpetrated perhaps the greatest British cultural atrocity. His dissolution of the monasteries was carried out in a needlessly wanton manner. What happened at Glastonbury was the worst example of the entire process. The elderly abbot, Richard Whiting, was set up on a blatantly false charge of treason. Along with two colleagues, he was sentenced to death. The King's Einsatz Kommando hit-squad stretched and tied the old man on a hurdle. This was dragged by a horse through the town, past the abbey, and up to the summit of the Tor, where gallows had been erected. There the three men were executed. Whiting's head was removed and placed above the abbey gate. The rest of his body was cut into four pieces that were displayed in nearby towns.

Geoffrey Ashe raised some disturbing points about the ghastly scenario in *King Arthur's Avalon*. It would require considerable effort, in wet and muddy November, for a horse to drag a man tied to a hurdle up to the top of the Tor. The construction of the gallows there was no easy task either. The summit is renowned for the strong winds that often blow across it. If the sole purpose of the deed was to instil fear in the population then why not choose the front of the abbey, in the middle of the town, where everyone could potentially see it? There's an unsettling hint of impractical stranger motives amongst the executioners. The three bodies strung up on a hill suggest a blasphemous parody of the crucifixion and archaic sacrificial rites.

The abbey library was trashed. Pages of priceless manuscripts were found as litter in the streets. The bones displayed as Arthur and Guenevere's were lost. Who knows what modern forensic science could have told us if they were still available? The monks were dispersed. Before long the majestic edifice of the building was pillaged for raw material. One of its later owners used explosives to blow great holes in the walls to satisfy his materialistic priorities. The Grail chalice of British Christendom disappeared, leaving a wasteland behind.

For hundreds of years Glastonbury seemed to go into a kind of suspended animation. At the beginning of the twentieth century the abbey ruins were put up for auction and passed into the hands of the Church of England. In 1908 a Bristol architect named Frederick Bligh Bond was placed in charge of archaeological excavations there. He was the ideal person for the task having considerable knowledge of medieval ecclesiastical architecture. He was also dedicated to the pursuit of secret knowledge that he believed was present in Christianity. A variety of clairvoyants with whom Bond was in touch, some of whom were not even in the country and knew nothing of Glastonbury lore, received some suggestive fragments hinting that, *"Our Abbey was a message in ye stones. In ye foundations and ye distances be a mystery." "All ye measures were marked plaine on ye slabbes in Mary's Chapell and ye have destroyed them." "In the designing of the Floor lies the future prophecy of Glastonbury, together with the inward secrets of Christianity."*

It was Bond who first stated the now widespread idea that numerical codes, suggestive of esoteric ideas, were embodied in the geometry of the abbey's design. The heavenly city of the New Jerusalem is depicted within a cube. Bond believed that just such a cube formed the basis for a major cosmological geometrical Qabalistic gnosis expressed in the abbey architecture.

Thanks to a triumph of barbarism over civilisation we don't have decorative carvings and statuary to lend themselves to Fulcanelliesque interpretations and that is a lamentable loss but Bligh Bond's astonishing work nonetheless helps Glastonbury Abbey to stand alongside Notre Dame and Chartres as an eternal beacon of esoteric Christianity.

Automatic writing was used to communicate with the collective conscious-ness of the departed monks, who referred to themselves as the "Company of

Avalon". They had, in a way, become part of the realm of Annwn. Directions for digging derived from such psychic sessions. A chapel mentioned in records but physically lost was located. Further good work followed. Boosted by his success, Bond was rash enough to reveal his methodology in the haunting book, *The Gate of Remembrance.*

He was eventually removed from his post. This extraordinary episode heralded the rebirth of Glastonbury. For those willing to consider such possibilities, the dynamic appeared to come from the invisible realms, from spiritual forces linked with the mysteries of Arthur and the Grail, Joseph of Arimathea and a whole host of saints. It gave hope that eventually, the horrors perpetrated by the syphilitic king and the profoundly bad karma of his national church, born in blood, could one day be annulled and transcended.

One piece of music has established itself for me as an ultimate soundtrack for a Glastonbury Abbey dream, in the process activating further my mysterious affinity for the idea of perpetual choir. It was *Spem in Alium* by Thomas Tallis (who had provided Vaughan Williams with such magnificent inspiration), a composition for forty voices. Tallis was writing during the aftermath of the dissolution of the monasteries and his work seems full of a poignant nostalgia for a lost paradise. I have cultivated the feeling that an eternal form of Glastonbury Abbey exists on some other realm of perception. There, the monks continue their daily services. A celestial choir perpetually intones sacred prayers amidst this magnificent scene, as Grail light shines through the stained glass windows, infusing the place with supernal blessings. *Spem in Alium* completely catches the feeling of how I believe such a choir would sound, like the chanting of angels. I know that the liturgical recitations of the medieval monks would not have sounded the same. It doesn't matter. Tallis takes me into a realm of unbearable beauty.

Tintagel of the Heart

R UDOLF STEINER visited Tintagel in 1924, not long before his death. As he gazed upon the castle ruins, his clairvoyant vision dissolved the barrier of time. He came to believe that Tintagel had once been a mystery centre in the manner of Eleusis. It supposedly dated from around 1100 BC. He wrote that,

> *"—Spirit power lies heavy round the mount,*
> *And mighty images of soul storm from the sea.*
> *The play of light and air rings magic changes,*
> *Which strongly penetrate the soul anew*
> *Even today, after three thousand years —"*

The fact that Steiner even visited the area in the first place was probably largely down to the one man who can be credited with virtually single-handedly reviving its Arthurian charisma and creating the modern tourist industry. Tennyson's *Idylls of the King* was a massive success whose immediate influence extended through decades. Such was the extraordinary effect on the area's fortunes that one wonders whether the poet was a reincarnated hierophant of the original mystery school returned to initiate a new cycle. Something seemed to be ripe and ready in the greater scheme of things.

The cliff top opposite the ruined fortress is dominated by the largest building in Tintagel, the hotel now named Camelot Castle. It seems as if the genius loci has decreed that a castle-like building of some kind needs to be strongly visible in that area. Originally built on the crest of the Tennysonian wave at the end of the nineteenth century, some of its rooms command views possibly as exquisite as any in the country. Over the years a cavalcade of diverse famous people have spent time there. Elgar had been inspired to write some of his second symphony. AA Milne, Noel Coward, and Winston Churchill make for an extraordinary mix. The fifties Arthurian Hollywood epic, *Knights of the Round Table,* had been partly shot in the area and Guenevere Ava Gardner had stayed, enjoying herself so much that she allegedly still haunts the place.

The most famous work of one of the leading figures of the great British

musical revival, Arnold Bax, was inspired by Tintagel. In the midst of
an intense love affair, he had spent an idyllic six week holiday at the hotel.
He was moved to compose a 'tone poem'. The fifteen minute piece tried
to evoke, *"the ruined castle, now so ancient and weather-worn as to seem
an emanation of the rock upon which it is built,"* with its Atlantic vista amidst
the lingering presence of the Arthurian mythos. Wind, sea, and legend
blend together. As someone who came to musical consciousness through
Rock A-Z, it took a bit of effort for me to get into it but it was well worth it.

Steiner and his small party, including the visionary artist Eleanor Merry
who had arranged the trip, spent some time at the big hotel as well. To the
modern mind, Camelot is a fortress of the imagination, of creativity and spirituality. The new castle that exists in the same physical space as the hotel can
serve that function. In an interesting continuity following through from
Steiner's theories on art and the importance of light and colour, the remarkable modern impressionist, expressionist, 'Abstract Realist', Ted Stourton
would later help establish Camelot Castle hotel as a matrix of creativity,
producing a gigantic corpus of work and encouraging others to come and do
likewise. Stourton and fellow hotel owners John and Irina Mappin honour
the awesome genius loci of the Tintagel of the Heart in the present day.

I find it astonishing that such a small area can be such a fount of inspira-
tional energy. At times in the summer, golden mists come off the sea and
render the castle island invisible. This is suggestive of an Avalonian otherworld. Jung had come to Tintagel and later had an important dream whilst in
India that seemed to reflect its influence. It featured a mysterious Grail
Castle-type island citadel. It was suggestive of a mandalic representation of
the structure of the Self.

I can imagine a timeless realm where a procession of illustrious people
who have visited the castle and Merlin's Cave walk amongst countless shades
back up the hill as golden mist and shadows ebb and flow around them.
Steiner, Jung, Hardy, Swinburne, Tennyson, Elgar, Bax, There was no way
Dion Fortune hadn't been there as well. She was amongst them.

During the period that Powys and Fortune were recognising certain qualities of the landscape of Glastonbury and helping to reawaken an accompa-
nying spirituality so Steiner's recognition of Tintagel's former spiritual function also helped to realign and reawaken it.

A powerful modern manifestation of this can be found in the middle of
the town. The Hall of Chivalry is a testament to the vision of one man.
Frederick Thomas Glasscock was a hugely wealthy partner in the custard
firm of Monkhouse and Glasscock. TV presenter Bob was a direct descendent of the other partner. Glasscock had an abiding passion for the Arthurian

mythos. After his retirement he had moved into a large house and made massive alterations to it in order to create a Hall of Chivalry. It was a major labour of love. Fifty types of stone from all over Cornwall were brought in for its reconstruction. Seventy two stained-glass windows were commissioned showing assorted heraldic devices and legendary scenes. The larger ones were of exceptional quality, worthy of a great cathedral. They were positioned in accordance with a precise scheme of colour that allowed rainbow light to fall upon the Hall. There were two round tables, a sword in a stone above an altar, and a throne.

Glasscock created a chivalric order, the Fellowship of the Round Table. Local men were initiated. Teenagers had a grade of Pilgrim. Younger children were Searchers, singing songs about the sagas. When the place was officially opened on June 5th 1933, five-hundred people attended. A musical programme included the Pilgrims March from Wagner's *Tannhauser*. The combination of sound, costume, and diffused coloured light must have been extremely effective.

Anyone with a taste for Arthuriana would have been aware of this Tintagel development. And that leaves uncomfortable possibilities hanging in the air. There were certainly Grail enthusiasts amongst the Nazis. At the beginning of that decade, before they even came to power, Rudolf Hess had despatched Dr Karl Hans Fuchs to Scotland to check out Rosslyn chapel, a location little known in those days for its esoteric potency. His mission is a matter of historical record for he lectured to the Edinburgh branch of the Theosophical Society during the visit. The Hall of Chivalry opened within six months of Hitler becoming chancellor. The new regime was looking for style models to assimilate.

In 1934 Himmler took control of a Schloss at Wewelsburg in Westphalia. He lavished immense time and resources in turning it into a Grail castle for his SS. People can argue about the extent of Hitler's occult interests and their effect on his career but with Himmler, there is no doubt of the matter. The SS were quite clearly conceived of as a modern chivalric order after the manner of the medieval Teutonic Knights. Schloss Wewelsburg was a place for their elite. It was a shrine to German history. There was actually a circular table there around which twelve men would gather. Ceremonies took place in the crypt that one can only speculate upon. It seems highly likely that processes of a meditational, ritualistic and occult nature were engaged in at least occasionally over a period of years. Once the war began this probably intensified. We don't have to go as far as Trevor Ravenscroft in *The Spear of Destiny* as to see Himmler as some empty shell manipulated by demonic forces, but the man's track record speaks for itself. Wewelsburg was his spiritual base. It was believed that many ley lines passed through it. This was where he and his associates like Reinhard Heydrich recharged their batteries. The thriller writer Duncan Kyle wrote a novel about Wewlesburg. It's a tale of espionage rather than occultism but its title evokes the magical reality: *Black Camelot*. I do wonder if Tintagel's Hall of Chivalry may have been a direct influence on Wewelsburg.

Glasscock died in 1934, en-route to America in an attempt to spread his Order, as Wewelsburg came into being. It seemed that his work was still-born, at least on the outer plane. Glasscock's Will bequeathed the Hall to the local Masonic Lodge of which he was a member. It was used by them and hired out for wedding receptions and so on. By the eighties the Masons only used it occasionally. It had become a gift shop and tourist attraction.

In my more mystical moments I have pondered on the possibility that Glasscock's attempt to found a new Order of Chivalry was a response to Steiner's impetus. He would probably have known of the visit. There is one work by Steiner and one about Anthroposophy in two bookcases full of old Arthurian volumes in the main hall. Anthroposophy considered itself to be a true Rosicrucian school. Glasscock was known to be keen on Rosicrucianism as well as Arthur.

The whole place seems to tremble on the edge of the etheric. I find it easy to intuit mystical nuances suggestive of vast spiritual forces at work there. It's like a chapter that got left out of *Spear of Destiny:* the Hall of Chivalry, alight with rainbow colours shining through visionary windows onto knights, pilgrims, and searchers, the air thick with incense and the rising sound of choirs, the whole scene hanging between Steiner's Goetheanum and Himmler's Wewelsburg. That's quite a mix to contemplate whilst watching a summer sunset near the castle ruins.

In Search of a
Primordial Wisdom Tradition

HAVING STARTED WITH LANDSCAPE and the distinctive 'personality' of Glastonbury and Tintagel, it is now time to see just how far it is possible to go from such beginnings. As well as Arthur the two locations appear to have something else in common. By a labyrinthine route though, we will establish some unity in diversity and be led back to Arthur and the Grail again.

One of the most notable visual aspects of Glastonbury Tor is the terracing on its slopes. On a sunny day it can be distinctly delineated by the play of light and shadow. A generally held theory contends that it derives solely from medieval agricultural practices. In recent times others have come to feel differently. Dion Fortune, who had a home in Glastonbury between the wars, wondered if the hill might have been deliberately sculpted in remembrance of a prototype holy mountain on some other continent. She had Atlantis in mind but the general idea would prove to be fruitful in later speculations.

In 1944, Geoffrey Russell had a mystical experience in Ceylon. In struggling to understand its meaning he produced a drawing of a pattern featuring various circles. He felt that it was something to do with the human brain. Nearly twenty years later he saw a picture of a small sevenfold labyrinthine maze design that had been discovered on a rock face near Tintagel and was considered to be perhaps three-thousand years old. He was stunned to recognise essentially the same design that he had drawn. This inspired him to undertake a study of the topic from both a historical and psychological perspective.

Mazes are most famously associated with Crete and the tale of the Minotaur. A particular maze pattern, known as 'Cretan' and septenary in form, of which the Tintagel case is one example, can be found in many places around the world.

The most striking result of Geoffrey Russell's journey of discovery was his theory that the Tor terracing is a unique three-dimensional form of the Cretan septenary maze design. Russell linked his postulated Tor maze to the famous Welsh Dark Age tale, *The Spoils of Annwn* where Arthur and his companions go in search of a wonder-working cauldron that seems to be a precursor of the medieval Grail. One of the featured locations is Caer Sidi. This is taken to mean the turning or spiral castle. Russell believes this motif shows a memory of maze-threading ceremonials. Somewhere in this mystery, the secret of the Grail waits to be revealed.

Jung had made much of the spontaneous production of sacred circle mandala-type designs by people undergoing transformational processes. He believed them to be symbols and expressions of the self in its deeper sense. The maze pattern was possibly an example of a similar manifestation. Are the widely separated mazes a spontaneous production of the human psyche, an archetype of Jung's collective unconscious, or can a physical cultural connection of some kind be discovered? Were Dion Fortune's idea of the Tor as a representation of a sacred mountain or temple prototype and Geoffrey Russell's maze theory mutually exclusive, or could they somehow have an underlying connection?

In two inter-related books, *The Ancient Wisdom* and *Avalonian Quest,* Geoffrey Ashe entered into an extensive consideration that helped to put the mystery of the seven-fold Glastonbury maze in a remarkable context of expanded perspective.

The starting point of Ashe's journey in *The Ancient Wisdom* is an investigation of the mystique of the number seven itself. The modern revival of occultism received its most powerful impetus from the Theosophical Society, founded in 1875 by the extraordinary Madame Blavatsky. Her major work, *The Secret Doctrine,* placed great significance on the number seven as a cosmic coding that pervades all of creation, revealing the pattern of the work of the divine. It was considered to be the supreme number of the higher mysteries. Why? Ashe pondered whether a potential source for its apparent prevalence might be located. If it could, perhaps a larger cultural package would then be identifiable as a genuine 'ancient wisdom'.

At first it seems that the Bible is the obvious reason for this. God made the world in seven days and therefore his chosen people structured their lives and culture around that, hence a seven-day week and so on. The presence of numerous sevens in the Old Testament shows the attempts by the Jews to align themselves with God's pattern of creation. This was picked-up on by the authors of the New Testament, in particular the *Book of Revelation,* where a septenary feast features fifty-four groupings of seven. All of this was then carried forward into the culture of the Middle Ages where it was commonplace to think of seven colours of the rainbow, notes of the musical scale, metals, archangels etc.

Jerusalem had been considered by the Jews to be the centre of the world.

It was literally the place where the process of creation began. The centre of the centre was Solomon's Temple. Everything about it was designed to embody divine laws. The ceremonies that took place within it didn't just reflect God's work, they helped to harmonise the world with it. They were necessary for the continuing existence of the world. These rites actually partook of the divine creative process. Without their proper performance a negative chaos would ensue and the world could even end. The presence in the temple of the seven-branched candlestick, the Menorah, affirmed the sacredness of seven. At the base of the temple was a rock that was supposed to be the first piece of solid matter made by God. This made it the navel of the world. Even stranger was the belief that the hill where the temple stood, known as Zion, was the highest point on Earth. This is particularly odd as the nearby, plainly visible, Mount of Olives is obviously taller. The world was considered to be flat and circular with a mountain at its centre. There are perplexing anomalous references to this mount in the Old Testament. Psalm 48, verse 2 refers to *"Mount Zion in the far north"*. Why the north?

Closer investigation reveals that the Babylonians had revered the number seven before the Jews. It seems that some of their ideas were passed on during the formative process of the writing of the Old Testament, in the time of the Babylonian captivity. Some academics argue that the Babylonian numerology stems from their knowledge of the planets, which they counted as seven. This list consisted of the visible planets of pre-telescope days, Mercury, Venus, Mars, Jupiter and Saturn with the addition of the Sun and the Moon. It seems however that the list was manipulated to align with an already established sacrality of seven. The Sun and Moon were not always included in planetary counts. Other cultures numbered them differently. The Chinese, for example, had five.

In Babylonian sacred culture seven appeared as part of a complex of closely connected concepts. In the city of Babylon was a circular 250 feet tall, seven-tiered ziggurat, known as the Etemenanki, *"the Temple of the Foundation of Heaven and Earth"* and the *"Mount of the Mountains of all Lands."* It was considered to be the centre of the world, the point of creation and its cyclic regeneration. On its summit was a temple where the climax of their New Year ceremonials, the *Akitu*, was acted out between the king and a priestess who represented the goddess. It was believed that through the ziggurat's centre ran a mystical axis, a 'bond' or binding post, connecting the realms of earth, underworld, and sky. The heavens rotated around its top. Here was one area though where there seemed to be a discrepancy between mythic and physical reality. Anyone standing on the top of the ziggurat and looking up to observe the sky could soon see that the pole star pivotal point was not directly above but off to the north. The world mountain temple seems to have been a model of an original located elsewhere.

Earlier Mesopotamian cities had similar ideas. Ziggurats had seven levels. The Sumerian capital Nippur's temple was known as the *"House of the Mountain"*. The city had a wall with seven gates. There were also significant sevens in the Sumerian Underworld, into which their "bond" or binding post, of cosmic unity extended. They feature in one of the most famous stories of the ancient world, the descent of the Goddess Innana who became the Babylonian Ishtar. She encountered seven judges at seven gates who demanded that she remove an item of clothing at each until she reached the heart of the underworld naked. The motif of the septenary path that reaches a centre by a difficult route suggests comparisons with mazes. Whilst the Sumerians clearly influenced the Babylonians, the mystery of the displaced centre of the heavens remains. The two cultures occupied essentially the same geographical region. The pivot of the sky would still be somewhere in the north.

Seven appears in the context of the sacred centre, the creation point, the heart of the world, both above and below ground, at Jerusalem, Babylon, Nippur and the Greek Delphi, which Ashe also examines in some detail in *The Ancient Wisdom*. It is not omnipresent throughout the ancient world but further examples of the familiar package of symbols do occur in some far-flung locations.

The idea of the world mountain as centre and starting point of creation is widespread in Asia. It is best known as the Mount Meru of Hinduism that has the familiar celestial pole star axis through its centre around which the heavens revolve. Remember that in Jerusalem and Babylon, the temples were not physically aligned in such a way, hence the need to somehow identify them with a prototype in the north and thereby partake of its archetypal potency. Meru was not believed to be located in India but to the north, where the migrating Indians had originated from. Ashe wondered if the references to *"Zion the far north"* were suggestive of a diffusion of a set of ideas from a point of origin connected to the Meru mythos.

Mount Meru has been portrayed with seven tiers. It is the home of the seven Rishis. They are human but endowed with divine qualities. These Masters of Wisdom are revealers of knowledge at the start of new cycles of history. They keep an eternal watch over the affairs of humanity. Blavatsky's Himalayan sages seem very similar. Gurdjieff's career was surely not unconnected.

In ancient times the polar constellation was Draco, the dragon serpent. The sky revolved around it. Finally, through looking at the heavens,

Ashe finds his source for the mystique of seven. It is in the seven stars of the constellation of Ursa Major, the Great Bear, considered to be the abode of the seven Rishis. Its stars circled about the centre of the sky and could be used to locate it. It therefore will always be in immediate proximity to the axis of the world mountain. Nations which had early versions of the sacred seven cultural package lived in latitudes where the constellation was always visible. It disappears in the later forms of Hinduism, as the Indians travelled south and it vanished from their sky. Ashe delivers detailed evidence of the significance of Ursa Major in many cultures down through the ages. The Sumerian Nippur was considered to align with it. Babylonians called it the bond of heaven.

Having travelled so far, Ashe has to acknowledge that Blavatsky was there before him. She does actually state that the first form of the sacred seven is visible in heaven as Ursa Major. She, in turn, derived this from the work of Gerald Massey who had said precisely that in his work, *The Natural Genesis*, published in 1883. The other associations he links to it are a very intriguing mix. He talks of Ursa Major being a visible symbol of a goddess. Artemis was born in the celestial circle that its movements traced around the polar axis. He also links the constellation with the world mountain and even the spiral labyrinth, specifically the so-called 'Cretan' form, which he claims, *"represents... the seven encirclers of the Great Bear"*. Massey's suggestion of the proto-myth behind this material is of a primal mythic mountain, *"the Mount of the Seven Stars... which represented the celestial north as the birthplace of the initial motion and the beginning of time."* On this seven-tiered Meru, the Great Goddess was enthroned. The world revolved around it and other sacred mountains were copies of it. Ashe marvels over the accuracy of Massey's insights and wonders how he may have come by them. They're all the more remarkable as Massey was a firm believer in the Egyptian origin of culture and primarily investigated its roots in Africa. Ashe is willing to concede that perhaps Massey had come into contact with some genuine occult tradition.

From looking at the associations of Ursa Major with bears, Ashe proceeds to the climax of his journey. He is led into the Siberian realms of the Altai mountain range, with its sacred Mount Belukha, and archaic shamanism. In this region can be glimpsed the oldest currently discoverable forms of the complete seven package. Mammoth ivory carved with seven circles of dots was discovered at an Altaic cave burial. Perhaps this was the first stirring of what evolved into the septenary maze design?

The early Hindus thought of Ursa Major as both the seven Rishis and the seven bears. Ashe recognised a kind of riddle here that seems to be asking, who can be both a bear and a seer? The answer is a shaman.

The shaman represents the earliest religious specialist. Generally speaking, the most powerful are born, not made. A series of common events in their early lives mark out a specific developmental syndrome. Intense psychic experiences may make normal life unbearable and force upon them a kind of dissolution of their personality. This can take the vivid form of dismemberment as limbs are torn asunder and fed to fierce demons. Some unfortunates never get beyond that. The ideal result sees the candidate put back together as a fully functioning shaman. They are able to demonstrate incredible abilities. In many cases they will carry the complete oral traditions of their tribes, memorising mythic sagas, plant lore, law codes and so on. They will act as mediators with the ancestors and deities. Most importantly their acceptance will be determined by their abilities to successfully function as healers and to help the tribe in their everyday tasks of hunting animals and generally finding food. The shaman will often magically identify with an animal and wear its fur and so on. It's all very well having weird experiences where you believe that you've left your body and can locate a lost animal or find a grazing herd for the hunters to attack, but if it doesn't turn out to be true they won't pay any further attention.

In the visionary world of the shaman can be found recurring motifs that are immediately familiar from the quest for the sacred seven. There is a world tree, an axis that connects the three realms of underworld, earth and heaven. It's sometimes pictured as a pole holding up the sky. The north star is pictured as immediately above. The shaman travels up and down it. It seems to be very much connected with the world mountain concept, with its levels and orientation to the pole star. This geography can be specifically internalised so that the shamans align their spinal columns with the world tree. The ascent of its different levels seems to prefigure the yogic chakra system. Mircea Eliade argued at length that yoga has clearly evolved from shamanic roots. Mount Meru was later located in esoteric texts as within the body of the yogi.

In the Altai region there are significant sevens associated with these three zones of the shaman's universe. In the underworld the lord of the dead lives at the bottom of seven levels with his seven sons and seven daughters. Geoffrey Ashe disagrees with authorities that believe the Central Asian shamans were influenced by India and Mesopotamia in their use of the world mountain and the number seven. He maintains that the transmission of ideas was in the opposite direction.

Shamanic lore often talks of a paradisiacal lost golden age when their powers were greater and humanity as a whole was closer to the divine. There are female shamans, and a case can be made that the most well known forms of shamanism may derive from a goddess-centred culture. It's an interesting fact that there is an established tradition of sex-change shamans. These are men who not only dress as women but live their whole lives as women and may marry a male. It's not a simple matter of homosexuality. It seems to reflect a belief that inspiration and magical power are importantly connected to the feminine.

The Altai region has also been the focus of another immense quest centred on the fabled realm of Shambhala. Somewhere in the mountains of Asia, perhaps in mysterious Tibet, was a valley where a group of sage immortals hid away from the world and engaged in secret great deeds for the good of all. Occasionally a worthy few would make contact with them.

Shambhala represents a living and vital reality for the Tantric Buddhists of Tibet and Mongolia, who believe it to be the home of a system of secret wisdom. Some of this is embodied in the teachings of the *Kalachakra*, which means 'Wheel of Time'. Its origins are believed to predate Buddha, who visited Shambhala himself to be initiated in its mysteries. On the one hand it has a tangible physical location but also strange qualities which can hide it from the profane, making it all but invisible to the outside world. Its pilgrims are somehow summoned by subtle inner means.

In some versions, this kingdom has a connected underground realm called Agharthi. There are traditions that an awesome being known as the 'King of the World' resides there. A remarkable story tells of how he actually appeared above ground and visited a monastery in 1890. He uttered a series of prophecies concerning a time of warfare and tribulation that was soon to come upon the world and would usher in *"a new life on the earth, purified by the death of nations"*. After this, the underground super-beings of Agharthi would rise up and claim the world. These prophecies were first published in the west between the wars.

During the nineteen-twenties there was a powerful belief in Central Asia that a time of an earthly kingdom of Shambhala was near. There were elements that a westerner could recognise from Christian millennial enthusiasms over the coming of the New Jerusalem. In a time of profound uncertainty in Asia following the Bolshevik revolution and the increasing power of Japan, Shambhala focused nationalist aspirations. A warrior lord was expected to lead the process. He was Gesar Khan. This hero of Tibetan and Mongolian myth cycles may have lived in the 8th century AD. A champion of righteousness, he had disappeared with a hint of return.

A legend of Gesar Khan told of him being sent seven heads that had been cut off from seven blacksmiths. They were boiled in seven kettles, which he made into seven chalices. A goddess-type figure then scatters them in the sky where they come to rest as Ursa Major. This tale seems to be full of archaic imagery suggestive of shamanism and the Altaic ancient wisdom package. So there is a living tradition seeming to originate around an area identified as a potential source for the seven mystique, the world mountain archetype and so on. The Great Bear and shamanism are common to both strands.

The Ancient Wisdom and Avalonian Quest also featured the work of the remarkable Stephen Jenkins, author of The Undiscovered Country, who had worked as a teacher in Mongolia and been initiated into a type of Tantric Buddhism that included Kalachakra Shambhala teachings. High-ranking Lamas told him that a European had visited Buddha. They believed him to be a Celt. He received Shambhalic initiation. In the midst of this mysterious episode the 'presence' of Shambhala was transplanted to Britain. Apparently the Lamas had been deliberating about the whole business for at least a century. They stated that Shambhala once had a literal physical existence in the Celtic Britain of the last centuries before Christ. In The Undiscovered Country Jenkins puts forward the possibility that it was actually Glastonbury. There's not exactly a lot of archaeology to back this one up but it is a marvellous mystical, poetic idea that sets the mind off on strange, suggestive tangents.

Ashe and Jenkins raise the possibility that something of the Central Asian ancient wisdom package made its way to Britain. The Glastonbury landscape seems to speak eloquently of it once the code is broken. The Tor combines many of the familiar motifs. The alleged septenary spiral maze appears to have sculpted it like a ziggurat. It could easily accommodate world mountain concepts. There seems to be an association of both paradise and underworld around it. The mythology of Arthur and his return is not unlike that of Gesar Khan. Ursa Major has been known as 'Arthur's wagon' and his very name is generally taken to mean 'Bear'. The Celts originated in Asia. Their Druid religious leaders evidenced definite shamanic elements.

With these considerations of Arthur, Ursa Major, and Glastonbury, Geoffrey Ashe's quest for an ancient wisdom can actually be expanded further still. There are others who would postulate that the Altaic Shambhalic zone is not actually the point of origin of the tradition but one step removed from it. Two of the twentieth century's most erudite esotericists, Rene Guenon and Julius Evola, were advocates of the concept of a northern polar centre that existed during an epoch when the climate there was conducive to a life that subsequent mythology has rendered as paradisiacal. This was a version of the Golden Saturnian Cronus age. The centre has various names in different traditions, the most common being Hyperborea and Thule.

Hyperborea is a famous mystery of classical literature. It was a land thus named because it lay beyond where Boreas the north wind blows. The place was a paradise sacred to Apollo. Numerous theories have been advanced as to its location. Geoffrey Ashe came out in favour of an Altaic shamanic source. Some have believed that the land of the Hyperboreans was Britain.

The Guenon/Evola esoteric hypothesis suggests a pole shift axial displacement resulting in a cultural drift to the south and west. The Altaic Shambhalic centre lay to the south. What became known as Atlantis reflected the westwards dispersal. Both of those subsequent centres influenced British and European culture from separate directions but the origins of both lay in the polar original. Far-fetched as this may seem, there is considerable evidence indicative of fundamentally different climate and conditions once existing in arctic regions that would have made the sustaining of an advanced culture there feasible.

With these ideas come nuances that impact on the concept of Arthur as an archaic deity who the Dark Age warrior became connected with. The fully developed form of his myth familiar from the Middle Ages portrays him very much as a solar figure. When glimpses of older material seem to be discerned though, he is seen by primal starlight. Anthroposophist Walter Johannes Stein stated that, *"Behind the historical figure of Arthur works a super-human spiritual being leading invisibly but most powerfully, the whole history of the island kingdom" "As the star-cluster of the Great Bear illumines the Pole and rules the hosts of the other stars, in like manner there gleams, amid the circle of the Round Table, the figure of King Arthur. In this Arthur circle we behold a brotherhood that is ordered according to the laws of the starry heavens."*

Lewis Spence, Rudolf Steiner, and Dion Fortune believed that Arthur was not a single individual but a kind of initiatory designation. In *New Light on the Ancient Mystery of Glastonbury,* John Michell portrays Arthur as a title that kings held down through the centuries from shortly after the last ice age. He would have been the earthly embodiment of a stellar deity. *"Arthur was the spirit guardian of those islands, the keeper of the Bear and also the leader of the bear hunt. His legendary adventures were ritually enacted as the tribes moved around the central pole of their territory, imitating the revolutions of the Great Bear around the pole star. Their totem was the bear; the image of their chief god was Arcturus and the Great Bear constellation, and the title assumed by their leader was Arth Fawr or Arthur".*

Michell was led to this idea through his investigation of the mystery of Glastonbury's seven holy islands. As far back as the Domesday Book, seven island hills in the Glastonbury area were given special legal status. They were free from taxation. The King himself had no power over them. The site of the abbey itself was one of them. The others were located at Beckery, Godney, Martinsea, Meare, Panborough and Nyland. Small chapels were placed upon these outlying hills, which the abbey maintained. The mystery is what was special about them. There are plenty of other hills in the vicinity and a number of them are larger. Looking at their position on a map, John Michell saw that they seemed to form the image of the constellation of Ursa Major. The Tor was the pole star Draco around which they revolved and may have been seen as Arthur's father, Pendragon, the dragon's head. It's a powerful idea, a possible glimpse of a Hyperborean ancient wisdom package, albeit it without any historical evidence to support it.

In *Lord of the World*, published in 1927, Rene Guenon gave a unique exposition of the Central Asian Agarttha/Shambhala ancient wisdom tradition. In the distant past many cultures had some kind of connection with Agarttha but the links were increasingly lost until in modern times they are only dim memories. *"The loss of the Grail, or of one of its symbolic equivalents, signifies the loss of tradition with all that this conveys. It is truer, in fact, to say that the tradition is hidden rather than lost, or to say that it can be lost only to lesser spiritual centres that have ceased to maintain a direct connection with the supreme centre."* The Grail quest tales speak in some way of the search to reconnect with it. Arthur himself represents the Lord of the World archetype.

One distinctive twelfth century mystery has been suggested as a possible sign of a Central Asian influence. During the same period that Arthur was becoming famous all over Europe and the conditions that generated the Grail romances were coming together, the figure of Prester John first came to prominence. He became known as a fabulously wealthy and powerful, hitherto unknown, Christian monarch of a kingdom located just beyond the known mental horizon of Europeans. Sometimes it was named as Ethiopia, although many didn't really have a clear conception of exactly where that was. 'India' became a general idea of Central Asia. Mysterious letters were received from Prester John by monarchs and dignitaries at the time. They were a great sensation as it suggested the possibility of aid in the crusades against Islam. In 1177, the Pope sent an envoy into Asia with a reply for the mysterious king. What became of this mission is unknown. It is clear that important people believed in Prester John's physical reality. Whatever the true roots of the Prester John stories, Guenon and Evola would consider him to represent the Lord of the World archetype and his kingdom to be a hint of Agarttha Shambhala, the functioning centre of the primordial tradition. With this comes the suggestion of some level of connection with Europe at this point in history.

Geoffrey Russell believed that the secret of the Grail was linked to the septenary labyrinth. When Geoffrey Ashe investigated the seven cultural package however, he never connected it with the Grail. Ashe gives Guenon a mention in passing, acknowledging that he represents another mysterious instance like that of Gerald Massey where someone displayed knowledge of many of the components of the postulated 'ancient wisdom.' Guenon makes much of Mount Meru, connecting it with Munsalvaesche, the Grail 'mountain of salvation' and gives Ursa Major a mention. Ashe doesn't comment on his Grail statements. The linking of the European Grail literature with the Central Asian Agarttha/Shambhala mystery is probably the most extreme form of an esoteric interpretation of the genre. If there are any links between medieval Europe and a Central Asian powerhouse of the primordial wisdom tradition the Sufis would probably be the intermediaries. Perhaps it was realigning an earlier connection, already millennia old. Needless to say, the kind of evidence that would satisfy any academic is completely lacking.

What cannot be doubted is that this same period saw enormous upheavals in Central Asia that seriously disrupted trading and cultural links with Europe. This was the time of the awesome Genghiz Khan who unleashed his Golden Horde of Mongol horsemen to conquer empires and destroy cities. If there were Masters of Wisdom in Asia then they would have needed to adjust their itinerary to accommodate the turbulence. Some would need to flee, others to go underground or to try and function within the new dispensation. One of the Khan's grandsons totally annihilated Baghdad in 1258. This has sometimes been lamented as one of the greatest cultural catastrophes in world history, the definitive triumph of barbarism. The glorious Arab civilisation of the time never fully recovered. Esotericists would suggest that the secret hierarchy had their hands full at this point. The energies that had been put into Europe were seriously needed elsewhere. Somehow they kept it together and in no time at all, thanks to their influence, the Chinese empire of another Genghiz grandson, Kublai Khan, became a legendary model of enlightened rule. Europe however, was put on the back-burner.

Remember the increasing motif in the Grail tales of its removal to India? The climax of *Later Titurel*, written towards the end of the thirteenth century and essentially the last of the major early medieval romances, with its elaborate depiction of the potentially Persian influenced temple, concludes with the Grail being taken to the kingdom of Prester John in India. Here was the process whereby, as Julius Evola put it, *"history departed again from what is higher than history"*.

Temple of the Stars

"Knowest though not Asclepius that our land is the image of heaven, the representation on Earth of every celestial ordinance? Our land is the temple of the world."

Asclepius
Corpus Hermeticum

THE MALTWOOD ENCHANTMENT

B LAVATSKY BELIEVED that in immemorial antiquity initiates of the primordial wisdom tradition had gone walkabout with some kind of zodiac package. There is a passage in *The Secret Doctrine* referring to a centre that one of these groups had established in the Gobi desert where *"the behaviour of the celestial bodies in the heavens were taken as a model, and the plan was carried out below on earth."* These ideas helped create the unique mindset of Katherine Maltwood who became responsible for perhaps the most contentious concept concerning Glastonbury.

Born in 1878 and receiving a fine education in world history and mythology, poetry, literature, history, art and architecture, music, painting, woodcarving and sculpture, she was fortunate to marry in 1901 a childhood friend, Oxford graduate John Maltwood. He became a wealthy businessman, gaining the unique distinction of inventing the *Oxo* cube. This enabled him to support his wife's interests and burgeoning career as a sculptress.

A period of extensive world travel, collection of artwork, and absorption of mystical literature followed. After the First World War, the Maltwoods bought a home at Chilton Priory, near the village of Chilton Polden in Somerset, within sight of Glastonbury Tor. It served as a base for their global travels, gradually becoming increasingly significant. Built in the nineteenth century in the style of the prevalent Gothic Revival, with castellated walls and a tower, it looks like some kind of ecclesiastical building but it's not. The place was full of genuine medieval relics acquired by its creator, the antiquarian and collector, William Stradling. There were bits and pieces from old churches in the vicinity, including floor tiles from Glastonbury Abbey. Frederick Bligh Bond was involved in its restoration and expansion.

Extraordinary inspirations came to Katherine in her study room in the tower. Gazing through enchanted scrying-glass windows out around the far-reaching panoramic view of the Somerset landscape, the inner vision of the mystic artist responded to subtle inspirations. Can we imagine the priory as a peaceful spring sunset silence settles across the landscape? A light shines from the windows of Katherine's tower, attracting our vision towards it. As we draw nearer, the room becomes visible. A woman sits with her back to us, reading at a desk. Coming closer we can see that the book rests over a large map spread out on the table underneath it. We can approach and look over her shoulder. Just what is it that has so thoroughly focused her attention? She's putting the book to one side and is staring intently at what is now revealed as a detailed map of the Glastonbury landscape. Taking up a pen, she begins to draw a shape formed by a river, roads, and field boundaries. A lion. She stops, sits back and stares at what she's done. Outside in the twilight, a soft breeze suddenly stirs. A few faint stars are becoming visible. The atmosphere has changed. Right out across the land beyond the priory, back in the direction of Glastonbury, something seems to ripple. Rising upwards, looking down and around, we can somehow discern shapes of light, stretched out in a vast circle. Some of them seem familiar. Are they signs of the zodiac?

In 1925 Maltwood was asked by the publisher Dent to produce a map to accompany a new edition of *Perlesvaus*. The work seemed to have a Glastonbury connection so the idea was for her to imaginatively use the local landscape to create an itinerary of the questing knights. Quite how the subsequent inspiration came remains unclear. There was an episode where a group of damsels await a knight who could clear a pass of a lion, *"so fell and horrible that never was none seen more cruel."* It kept getting killed but still returned. The lion has heraldic associations. It was the epoch of King Richard the 'lion heart' who supposedly introduced the beast to our coat of arms. It appears in a number of Arthurian tales. There's nothing obviously unusual about its appearance at first glance.

The lion was somewhere in the back of her mind as she scanned maps of the area. Something about a particular configuration of varying features attracted her attention. It seemed as if a vast leonine form, three miles long, was emerging from the landscape. Somerton, once the Saxon royal capital of Wessex, lies between its paws. The place seems to have lingering solar associations appropriate to a lion connection. There is indeed a Red Lion

pub in the town. In a wooden roof within St Michael's church, medieval balls
have been found from a time long pre-dating the formation of the Football
Association. The roots of the national game are suggestive of archaic rites
where the ball represented the sun. An ancient road named Somerton Lane
delineates the lion's back. Copley Wood covers the top of his head, serving
as the mane. The ribs and front part of its hind leg are outlined by the River
Cary, the nose, mane, and tail by streams that run into it. Raised earthworks
shape the jaw. A red-earthed footpath supposedly shows its tongue. Lions'
claws have been excavated from Romano British graves near Charlton Adam,
which lies at the rear of the figure. This bizarre combination of elements was
enough to convince Katherine Maltwood that the huge lion was really there
and that the author of *Perlesvaus* knew of it in some way. The four main hero
figures featured, Arthur, Gawain, Lancelot and Perceval may represent the
four seasons of the sun. Their adventures could occur over a very specific
landscape. Recalling the presence of other strange creatures in the narrative,
she went back to it with fresh eyes. She later recalled the moment in *The
Enchantments of Britain*. "*Obviously, if the lion was a nature effigy then the
dragon, griffon and the giants etc, must be likewise; perhaps this was the most
thrilling moment of my discovery.*"

Guided by the same kind of combination of topographical features that
had revealed the lion, and some advice from an astrologer friend, Katherine
Maltwood went on to find a sequence of similar landscape figures that
apparently represent a complete zodiac with a circumference of about thirty
miles. Included were the usual ram, fishes, and a scorpion for example. The
apparent symmetry of the design seems impressive. Firstly, we have zodiacal
images in correct sequence pivoting around a central point. The heads of
all but one image face west. Winter signs are placed in the north, four of
which are partly drawn by the River Brue, summer signs lie in the south, four
drawn with the aid of the River Cary. Eight of the effigies are similar in size,
approximately 6,000 yards in breadth. There are three human figures in
the group, Sagittarius, Virgo, and Gemini, which are taken to represent
a father mother and child trinity and form an equilateral triangle. If laying
a planisphere of the same scale as the landscape zodiacal circle down upon a
map, the stars of the various constellations do tend to lie within the bounds
of the alleged effigies. This enables one to say that a particular star has a
definite corresponding location on the ground. This is the Hermetic
'As above, so below' par excellence. Primarily the configuration has come
together through some extraordinary process in nature that has been
recognised and then enhanced through human agency.

Maltwood concluded that this Glastonbury zodiac was the true round table of Arthur. The king himself was part of it, as the mounted archer of Sagittarius. Here was his original titanic form, asleep in Avalon. It was the Arthur figure that helped Maltwood to determine when the mighty work was constructed and by whom. Sagittarius has been variously linked with assorted ancient deities whose names seem similar to Arthur: ie Assyrian Assur, Persian Ahura, and Phoenician Melkarth. Glastonbury's Sagittarian archer seems to have a bearded face and pointed cap suggesting a middle-eastern look. He is aiming directly at the star Aldebaran, in Taurus. The Mesopotamian rivers Tigris and Euphrates rise at the spring equinox. Today the sun enters Aries at that time. When, due to precession of the equinoxes, it had been in Taurus, Aldebaran was synchronised with the rivers as Sirius once was with the Nile inundation. It began the Babylonian New Year festivities that were regulated by Marduk. Katherine Maltwood came to believe that it was during this period, around 2,700 BC, that the landscape zodiac was constructed by wandering initiates of some Middle Eastern mystery cult.

One considerable difference between the Glastonbury design and conventional zodiacs served as further evidence to Maltwood of its Babylonian provenance. The Aquarian effigy is supposedly in the shape of a phoenix. This figure looms all the more prominently due to its linking with Glastonbury's most notable landmark, the Tor, forming most of its head. The bird holds the Chalice Well in its beak! Maltwood mentions the tale of the Chaldean bird Zu who forced entry into the chamber of destiny and seized the tablets of fate. Zu was taken to represent Aquarius.

The most notable of all design differences comes with the absence of any depiction of Cancer. In its place is a ship representative of the nearby constellation of Argo Navis. This vessel is of considerable significance to the general design and the mysteries it embodies. It corresponds to the Grail romance Ship of Solomon. Details of the vessel and its narrative importance vary in the romances. It makes a brief appearance in Robert de Borron's work. Chretien has it drawn by a swan. The *Prose Perceval* has it steered by a bald elderly man. It features briefly in *Perlesvaus*. There's more detail in the *Quest Del Saint Graal* though. Sailing in the Glastonbury landscape version is the divine child of Gemini. The masts of the vessel converge at the Zodiac's central point.

Perhaps the most convincing of all the effigies is not actually part of the zodiacal twelve. There is supposedly a guardian dog of the sacred round table. Its nose is at Burrow Mump, a kind of mini-Tor that some have speculated may be artificial, also with a ruined Michael church on its summit, that forms part of John Michell's famous Michael ley. The nearest town of any size is Langport. An old Somerset song tells how

"The Girt Dog of Langport has burnt his long tail
And this is the night we go singing Wassail".

'Girt' means large. An impressive number of evocative place names cluster
around the area where Maltwood saw the effigy. His tail is at Wagg! There
are two Head Droves near his head, Earlake Moor by his ear, *Cur*ry Rivel on
a front paw. Even if a huge effigy doesn't exist, these are strong indications
of some kind of dog tradition in the vicinity.

Maltwood believed that the author of *Perlesvaus* was a Templar and was
convinced of their presence and influence in early medieval Glastonbury.
In accordance with general occult lore, she accepted that their mysteries
influenced the Rosicrucians. Both groups were considered to be part of
the infinitely older mysteries of Freemasonry, of which Maltwood had a
long-term interest. She believed that the Craft had ancient roots in Middle
Eastern cultures and included some knowledge of the stellar gnosis she was
uncovering around Glastonbury. The Gemini figure had an arm raised at
an angle suggestive of a Mason's square. Their lost word was analogous to
the Grail. She was initiated into a female lodge during the period of her
Glastonbury research.

In *A Guide to Glastonbury's Temple of the Star,s* published in 1935, and
The Enchantments of Britain, published in 1944 after a move from Britain to
Canada, Katherine Maltwood put forward her ideas on the Glastonbury
Zodiac and its connection with *Perlesvaus.* A set of aerial photos were also
taken for a now rare companion volume. Like Alfred Watkins' *Old Straight
Track,* academics scarcely registered Maltwood's works. British occultists of
the time don't seem to have been particularly aware of her either.

Temple of the Stars did find prestigious support amongst the most elitist
of the contemporary European occult cognoscenti. In his short essay,
The Land of the Sun, Rene Guenon suggested that some of the divergences
from the usual zodiacal designs were actually a point in favour of the archaic
authenticity of the Glastonbury configuration. Libra is represented by a
dove, rather than the usual scales. The bird is placed near the centre of
the design at the summit of the converging masts of the Argo Navis ship
and could be taken to appear as if flying from the Arthur figure's head. The
actual stars of Libra do not fall on the effigy but those of Ursa Major do.
Guenon noted that, *"the celestial scales were not always zodiacal, but were at
first polar, the name having been applied originally to the Great Bear, or to
the Great Bear and Little Bear taken together."* The axial alignment of the
Glastonbury Zodiac is polar. The stars of Ursa Major and Draco the sky
serpent, home of the former pole star, are found around its centre.

Once again Glastonbury is conceived as an outpost demonstrating certain motifs of a prior package. Ashe postulated the World Mountain, the maze and the number seven as the giveaway code. Guenon was likewise an advocate of the World Mountain but saw in the Maltwood revelation some of his own significant signs. Probably prompted by the attention of his one-time mentor Guenon, Julius Evola also accepted the Zodiac, stating in *The Mystery of the Grail* that, *"Glastonbury was itself in prehistoric times a centre of the primordial tradition."*

MARY CAINE AND THE DRUIDIC COSMOLOGY

In 1950 Ross Nichols, later to found the Order of Bards, Ovates, and Druids, wrote an article on *The Great Zodiac of Glastonbury* for the *Occult Observer*. He noted the presence of what he considered to be Druidic motifs and teachings within the Somerset design. Much of this had already been noticed by Katherine Maltwood but Nichols gave it greater emphasis. The father mother divine child trinity was considered particularly important. Most notable of all was the multiple meanings in the Gemini design. The child in the boat with the converging three masts and dove whose body and wings seem to reiterate the arrowhead symbol at their apex appeared to represent a complex glyph full of Druidic teachings. The deity Hu Gadarn saw three pillars of light in which were contained all divine knowledge. Three converging pillars became an ideogram of God's name, in a similar manner to the Hebrew Tetragrammaton.

A problem here is that a lot of material accepted by various Druid orders has similar controversies to the Hermetica surrounding it. Age and authenticity are topics of constant contention. Nonetheless, the teachings are mystically and magically potent. Druids are a kind of archetype of the western collective unconscious with Merlin their prime embodiment. The very word, along with Witch, can set people off on extraordinarily fertile chains of association and creativity. Just as the constant evolution of the Arthurian mythos is a measure of its power and durability so likewise the aura of the Druid shines brightly. If we look solely at the Dark Age Arthur or the Druids portrayed by Caesar we may be missing the point. Combine the two with Glastonbury and you would be best prepared by accepting that the journey will be one in an exalted realm where myths are born, poems created and symphonies heard, where visions of zodiacal figures emerge from the landscape.

In 1961 artist Mary Caine joined the London Order of Druids. It was in such company that she first heard of the Glastonbury Zodiac. Initially sceptical, she decided to write to Katherine Maltwood in Canada with detailed questions. She received a reply from John stating that his wife had died just three months before. It was at the same time that Caine had first heard of her work. There was a sense of synchronicity. Mary came to feel that in that period of time, the work was in some sense handed over to her to carry on. Accompanied and supported by her husband Osmund, who was also an artist, she became a tireless champion of the landscape enigma. The couple never lived in Glastonbury but spent extensive time in the area.

From the mid-seventies to early eighties, Mary Caine promoted her pamphlet, *The Glastonbury Giants*, and full-length book, *The Glastonbury Zodiac: Key to the Mysteries of Britain*. The Caines also created a charming video. Featuring Vaughan Williams' *Fantasia on a Theme by Thomas Tallis*, it plays as a quintessential piece of Earth Mysteries, an impressionistic poetic evocation of British Music. It probably didn't get much exposure on archaeology courses.

True to her roots, Caine emphasised Druidic aspects of the Zodiac, alongside the more distinctly Arthurian ones. She took her exegesis into realms that would have pleased the British Israelites. This group, whose heyday had been in the nineteenth century, tended to believe that the Celts had been the Lost Tribes of Israel. Caine also makes much of Wearyall Hill, the fabled location for Joseph of Arimathea's visit at the start of the Piscean Age. The hill is one of the Pisces fishes and therefore the perfect place for such a mission to help key in the coordinates for the Christian epoch.

The most famous aspect of Mary Caine's work was her noticing through aerial photography a most remarkable configuration of woodland on Dundon Beacon that looked like a conventional face of Christ. The fact that it happened to lie over the exact area already identified as the head of the Gemini being rendered it all the more peculiar. It has become the most widely distributed image connected with the Glastonbury Zodiac. Mary Caine was inevitably drawn to refer to Blake's question, *"did the countenance divine shine forth upon our clouded hills?"* It was also notable that the very peak of the hill, where beacon fires had once been lit, was the area on the effigy's head where the yogic third eye was situated. The name of the Druidic bard Taliesin meant 'radiant brow' and this seemed to fit the general mythic mix of the Gemini figure very well. In recent years the trees have been cleared and the image no longer exists.

REALITY CHECK

It is worth pausing to take stock of some of the diverse elements present in the brew and address consensus concerns. To begin with, we have the Maltwood interpretation of *Perlesvaus*. Much ink has been expended by critics in search of an understanding of this distinctive text but a zodiacal aspect had yet to be expounded by the time of *Temple of the Stars*. If it is really there, it's buried pretty deep. It may well be that the author was working with strands of assorted tales that contained sub-texts the meaning of which he was unaware. There are a number of big events in the story that the Maltwood/Caine corpus conveniently ignore. The fifteen hundred people getting their brains bashed out with giant hammers and the drowning in a vat of blood and suchlike don't feature much in the zodiacal exegesis. The hostile critic can be forgiven their scepticism.

Maltwood mentions that the *Quest del San Graal* stated enigmatically that, "*The Round Table was constructed, not without great significance, upon the advice of Merlin. By its name it is meant to signify the round world and round canopy of the planets and the elements in the firmament, where are to be seen the stars and many other things.*"

It also mentions the table of the Grail feeding four thousand people and 150 bulls. It was '*in a meadow*'. This does seem to clearly indicate that it covers a large area on the land. It might have been more useful for Maltwood's argument if *Perlesvaus* said something similar so clearly but the quote does hint at strange ideas about the Round Table existing somewhere in the background around the beginning of the thirteenth century.

The first mention on the Round Table comes in the *Roman de Brut* of Wace. This was a translation into French of Geoffrey of Monmouth that included considerable additional material, the Round Table being the most notable. Where Wace got the idea from is yet another area of constantly conflicting theories. Perhaps it derived from Celtic tales circulating amongst the Bretons. Maybe it was inspired poetic invention?

In the Grail romances and historical documents of the period there are three meanings for the term Round Table. One is the most obvious, a table to eat a meal from. It also means a chivalric institution, an order of knighthood. In that context it will tend to mention large numbers of people. Wace uses both designations. Taken as a whole, the Grail romances use the term Round Table to describe an institution more often than an eating place, although that's not how later times remember it. The third meaning is that of a tournament of some kind, a pageant, a show, an invocation of chivalry, featuring jousting and feasting. These gatherings were often inspired by the

Arthurian mythos. The famous Winchester Round Table may well have been constructed as an accompaniment to such an event. This could be sufficient explanation for the seemingly odd romance references.

Scholars of Maltwood's time believed many things about British pre-Roman history that would now be called into question. Many of her apparently wild theories arose out of such a background of ideas. For example, in *Enchantments of Britain,* she quotes LA Waddell from his *Origin of Britons and Scots* who claimed that the Welsh originated in Sumeria. *"We discover that the 'Cymry' of Wales derive their name from 'Sumer'.* Various traders and colonisers had come to ancient Albion by about 2700 BC. The Celtic Caer Sidi starlore was a mutated form of the Mesopotamian cultural package. This was a variant on widely stated beliefs of the time. The reputable Arthurian scholar John Rhys (who Powys used extensively for researching his great novel) considered that Somerset meant 'Land of Summer'. Druidic material of debatable authenticity spoke of the Cymry being led from the east, from a *"Summer Country over the hazy sea".* If that wasn't discouraging enough it is a tad unfortunate that one of Waddell's most used words is 'Aryan'. He is in fact so enthusiastic in his advocacy of it that his works are popular today amongst mystics whose sensibilities could be described as somewhere to the right of centre.

So what was happening in Somerset round about the period when wandering Sumerians are supposed to have disembarked circa 2700 BC? There was certainly a lot going on in the area by Neolithic times. Trees were being cleared using axes made from stone seemingly imported from distant locations. Wooden trackways crossed the Somerset Levels through the marshland. These constructions constitute what are essentially amongst the oldest roads in the world, having been individually dated to periods between 3806 to about 2500 BC. The tracks had a limited lifespan and were primarily for use during the more flooded times of the year. Cattle were driven across them. Canoes docked at the ends of some. The culture that produced them was obviously well organised and with manpower resources. The people were not isolated. They had contact with the world beyond. Somewhere in the middle of that timescale the Sumerian genesis of civilisation with the wheel, writing, decimal counting etc, can be dated. The famous lake villages were some considerable time later, a few hundred years BC only.

The Sumerians were also pioneer seafarers but could they possibly have travelled as far as Britain? There is a total absence of any archaeological proof here. Even the idea that Egyptians could have travelled the same way a millennia later is hugely contentious. A few Egyptian artefacts have been discovered in Britain but it has been generally considered that they arrived via middlemen and it doesn't mean direct contact. The best that can be said is that the current absence of proof for Sumerian travellers cannot be equated with impossibility.

If they did travel to Somerset they would have found a landscape significantly different from today and this has a major bearing on the Zodiac theory. The issue of the Argo Navis vessel represents the best case in point. It's unique in the Glastonbury Zodiac for a number of reasons. Of all the effigies it's the only one that depicts a man made object, the rest are animals or humans. It contains straight lines, a feature obviously not found in nature. That implies that, assuming the thing is actually there in the first place, it must have been engineered by humans rather than being some mysterious artwork of Gaia. The problem is that the whole area was marshland until the period from 1790 to 1820. The moors were then drained and rhynes built across the flat area. It's those rhynes that define the ship, so it wasn't there in the medieval period and certainly not in Sumerian times.

A strange local custom gives pause for thought though. In nearby Minehead an inverted boat is dressed as a horse. This apparently commemorates a phantom ship that entered the harbour without anyone on board in the distant past. Earth Mysteries advocates will suggest that a location can influence the creativity of its inhabitants. The people who laid out the rhynes to form the ship needn't necessarily have had a clue about what they were doing. Strange forces simply prompted them to conform to a latent pattern. Perhaps, millennia ago, some impressive vessel really had sailed into the vicinity, leaving an indelible trace in site memory.

Both Maltwood and Caine made the dangerous leap of logic that all references to zodiacal lore in British mythology derive from the Glastonbury Zodiac. It simply doesn't follow that a reference to the stars in Welsh literature encodes the Glastonbury gnosis handed down through Druidic initiates.

Geoffrey Ashe has always maintained a certain scepticism about the Zodiac. First and foremost, he simply can't see the figures in the land even when they're pointed out to him. He has wondered if an experimental control group were shown various aerial photos of the British landscape that included the Temple of the Stars but were not identified as such that anyone would spontaneously pick out the image of a lion or a boat. Katherine Maltwood was a sculptress after all. She was predisposed to seeing potential shapes in things.

I consider the point to be a valid one. How many people, not already familiar with the Zodiac hypothesis, when seeing an image of the Tor, would say it looked like a phoenix? Some might compare it to Mesopotamian or Mexican step pyramids. The vast majority I'm sure, if pressed to liken it

to anything, would probably opt for symbolism of the female form. Local
RAF pilots refer to the Tor tower as the 'nipple'. The Pre-Roman cultures of
our islands often linked rolling hills and summits with Goddess figures. It is
ideas of this kind that have found far wider response in recent times.

Geoffrey Ashe himself can take some credit for inspiration that amounts
to more than a mere suggestion. In *The Finger and the Moon* the Wild Hunt
sequence segues into a numinous vision of a vast primordial goddess figure
whose body is made from the Glastonbury landscape. She stands up,
"ten thousand feet tall" and walks. Another form of the vision is repeated in
Avalonian Quest. In *The Goddess in Glastonbury*, Kathy Jones expanded the
basic configuration whereby, *"the side-view of the Isle of Avalon presents the
profile of a giant Goddess lying down lengthways"*. *"Stonedown is the head of
the Goddess, sinking back into the landscape. The Tor rises up as Her left
breast and Her ribcage. Chalice Hill is Her pregnant belly. Bere Lane marks
Her hips and Wearyall Hill is Her left thigh and leg, Her foot sinking into the
ground towards the nearby town of Street."*

Priestess of Avalon

MORGAN'S CAULDRON

THERE IS NO HISTORICAL DOCUMENTATION or archaeology to definitively link Glastonbury with any Goddess cult but the inferential reasoning is strong. The idea seems to express yet another quality of the personality of the place that has returned to collective awareness in accordance with some arcane timescale. Powys was an early articulator of it when, as we have seen, he said that *"ages before any saint or Saviour of our present Faith appeared in Glastonbury — the earth-goddess had her cauldron of the food of life safely guarded in our Island of the West."* The climax of his great novel sees a flood that returns Glastonbury to its primordial state of female shaped hills rising out of primal waters. It is then that the most fundamental vision of the Grail reveals itself as an expression of the divine feminine. *"Out of the Timeless she came down into time. Out of the Un-named she came down into our human symbols. Through all the stammerings of strange tongues and murmurings of obscure invocations she still upholds her cause; the cause of the unseen against the seen, of the weak against the strong, of that which is not, and yet is, against that which is, and yet is not."* The divine feminine, *"moves through the generations from one twilight to another; and of her long journeying from cult to cult, from shrine to shrine, from revelation to revelation, there is no end."* She brings *"the breath of what is beyond life and beyond death; and none, but such are covenanted as her own, discern her goings and her comings"*.

A Glastonbury Romance was written and published during the same period that Dion Fortune was active in the town and preparing the material that was published as *Avalon of the Heart* in 1934. Powys' novel had generated a lot of controversy in the town and Fortune makes a few disparaging remarks about it in her work. A greater unity however can be glimpsed beyond any apparent divergence.

During the thirties, it seems that what occultists would term "inner plane" events were in motion that led to the post-war rebirth of witchcraft and the general return of the Goddess. Perhaps the first stirrings had come when Egyptologist Margaret Murray was staying at the Chalice Well, Glastonbury's cauldron of Morgan, in 1915. A conversation there concerned the idea that the witch cult suggested by the medieval trials was an authentic pagan survival. This set Murray off on the path to her contentious works that helped inspire the modern witchcraft revival.

It is entirely appropriate that such a stimulus should arise at a location associated with Britain's most famous sorceress. Half-sister of Arthur, Morgan is characterised in the early medieval Arthurian literature as Queen of the faery realm of Avalon in the Celtic otherworld. She is a shapeshifting sorceress and healer, learned in starlore and mathematics, a female Merlin Druidess. By the time of Malory at the end of the Middle Ages, her character had been thoroughly assassinated. Helen Mirren's portrayal in *Excalibur* typifies her general depiction as a scheming manipulative malevolent figure, largely responsible for the doom that befalls the King.

Numerous models have existed for the male magician magus-type. From the Middle Ages to Crowley, there was a certain way of being, a particular style that the would-be adept could take on board. For women it was different. The burning times had left unfavourable archetypes associated with witches. If the figure of the Priestess was to return, somehow she needed to be rehabilitated, restored to the fullness of her functions. People had to have an idea in their heads of what such a figure would be like and how she might feel and behave in the modern world.

Dion Fortune wrote two occult novels set in the thirties, *The Sea Priestess* and *Moon Magic*, that featured the character Vivien Le Fey Morgan, who became Lilith Le Fey Morgan. The names combined two notorious women of the romances. Vivienne had led Merlin to imprisonment. Fortune's portrayal of the characters expressed a good deal of her own idealised magical personality, in the process embodying the qualities of the Arthurian sorceresses, but in a way that revitalised their mystery, expanding what they represent and opening up vistas that speak of a lineage of profound antiquity.

There is an implication that the two are fragmented aspects of a primordial original. Fortune felt that the Celtic myths contained layers of ancient material not native to Great Britain. Arthur, Merlin and Morgan were not solitary individuals but titles passed down through the ages from lost Atlantis. Adept refugees from the sunken continent found their way to Albion and introduced their Pendragon mysteries to the indigenous peoples. Cornish folklore of lost Lyonesse carries an echo of this. The tale of Merlin's magical overseeing of Arthur's conception refers to a genetic experiment to crossbreed the Atlantean stock of Igraine with the royal Celtic blood of Uther. Obviously there is no history to back this up and it may strike many as a very strange idea but some have felt some strange haunting truth there that again gives a hint of that elusive *something*.

Bringing forth the Priestess figure helped pave the way for the return of the witch and the Goddess. Being as her fictional magical women had Arthurian connections as well, this linked in with another of Dion Fortune's most important concerns. The Arthurian mythos had been greatly revived by poets and painters during the nineteenth century. Fortune was trying to revive it in a different way. She believed that it is possible to work with the collective mind of a race through the magical use of its mythic archetypes. Geoffrey of Monmouth had talked of Morgan receiving Arthur at the Avalon that became identified with Glastonbury. The same process of association can lead to the assumption that Glastonbury is likewise the realm of Morgan and her associated women. Dion Fortune had helped to activate an archetype. In the climax and greatest test of her life and work something of the power of the idea of Morgan at Glastonbury presiding over a return of Arthur possibly helped give her energy and inspiration when it was most needed.

FINEST HOUR

Remarkable events occurred during the Second World War that I have come to feel represent Glastonbury's finest hour so far. It seems strange to me that they are not better known. To any occultists of the time it was obvious that the Nazis were making use of magical techniques. They had helped to mobilise a nation's consciousness through the manipulation of folklore and mythology. The energy unleashed by this was immensely powerful and had easily swept all before it. Dion Fortune felt that a British response was urgently needed. We had plenty of traditions of our own that could be invoked. The mediocrity represented by years of appeasement and non-entities like Neville Chamberlain needed to be transcended. What followed was a new departure in the history of magic.

Shortly after the start of the war, letters were sent out every week to a group of associates across the country. They contained details of visualisation meditations that were to be carried out in unison every Sunday morning. The focus became Glastonbury Tor. Imagery gradually built up over a period of months. The participants would find it coming to life and developing of its own accord. Feedback would be exchanged and this would influence the next sequence. It was believed that messages from discarnate sources were received.

To begin with, the scene consisted of a large cavern inside the Tor. A red rose on a cross of gold hung in the air. For those initiated in the Golden Dawn tradition this was seen as a more detailed glyph covered in magical

symbols. Three rays of light, red, purple and blue, emanated from a point
above and behind the cross. The fully developed form of the imagery saw
Christ at the apex of the converging rays. The purple light was central,
reaching down behind and beneath the cross. At its base could be seen the
Virgin Mary, holding a chalice. The red beam came down at an angle to the
left of the cross and culminated in an image of Arthur, sitting on a white horse
and holding Excalibur aloft. To the right of the cross, the blue ray projected
a vision of Merlin, holding an orb of sovereignty. The imagery was arranged
over the broad schemata of the Qabalistic Tree of Life, a design and philosophy
that Fortune had written a whole book about, it having formed the basis of
her magical education.

To me, it seemed a very powerful equilibration of Britain's pagan and
Christian heritage. When it mattered, they functioned from a space of unity.
From this inner plane realm, spiritual forces streamed through into the soul
of the nation fortifying it against the potent will of Nazism. That's what Dion
Fortune and her associates believed and my temperament inclines me to
agree with them.

My sense of that time has been hugely expanded by the unbearably
poignant powerful feeling of the Tor as the spiritual heart of the nation, from
where the guardians of the Grail fought the forces of darkness. Wewelsburg
could be thought of as a kind of antithesis of Glastonbury, its polar opposite.
I don't know whether British occultists had any knowledge of the Black
Camelot. There is no mention of it in Dion Fortune's published letters of the
period. It does seem that the Nazis managed to keep the place secret. How
appropriate that the Tor, our British inner plane Grail castle, situated in a
landscape imbued with Arthurian associations, functioned as the focus of
spiritual resistance.

There are strong implications of another bit of hidden history here as
well. Knowing the Nazi interest in the Grail as proven by the scale of Himmlers'
castle restoration, which could conceivably have been influenced by
Tintagel, Fuchs Rosslyn mission and Otto Rahns' extensive investigation of
Cathar territory that was eventually funded by the SS, it seems a safe bet that
Glastonbury would have been checked out in the thirties. One wonders if
there may have been an occasion when Dion Fortune, moved by some
psychic intuition of unease, looked up from pruning her roses in Chalice
Orchard to note some unknown but somehow disturbing individual walking
past in the direction of the Tor.

Dion Fortune was not the only Avalonian to contribute to the inner plane
war effort. Wellesley Tudor Pole was responsible for securing the Chalice
Well gardens for future generations. He had profound connections to

Glastonbury's mysteries including the story of the Blue Glass Bowl covered superbly in Patrick Benham's *The Avalonians*. In 1917, during the First World War, he was on active service on the middle-eastern front, the same area that Lawrence of Arabia was involved in. He and a fellow officer were camped at the mouth of a cave near Jerusalem, preparing for likely fighting the next day. Their conversation took a profound direction. Tudor Pole's colleague stated that he was sure he would not survive the conflict. He suggested that Tudor Pole would live to see a greater war in the future. He asked that when that time came the fallen of the earlier war should be remembered. Wherever they were they would have a part to play. *"Give us the opportunity to do so, for that war for us will be a righteous war. We shall not fight with material weapons then, but we can help you if you will let us. We shall be an unseen but mighty army. — You will still have 'time' available as your servant. Lend us a moment of it each day and through your Silence give us our opportunity"*. The next day the man was killed.

In the days following the Dunkirk evacuation, what he had said was remembered. Tudor Pole was able to help instigate a daily minute of national silent prayer. This was fully supported by the King and government. The BBC incorporated it into their schedule in such a way that later in the year, beginning on Remembrance Sunday (when the dead of the First World War were most obviously acknowledged), a chime of Big Ben at nine pm gave the signal for the silent minute to begin. Many in occupied Europe listened to the BBC and adhered to the silent minute as a potent communion and prayer for victory. Such was its popularity that the practice was continued until 1961. It has been revived again at the Chalice Well gardens in recent years.

People who belittle Glastonbury as a place of meaningless fantasy would do well to consider the contributions of Dion Fortune and Wellesley Tudor Pole to the spiritual morale of the nation in 1940. I see clear indications of the tremendous vitality of Glastonbury and its role as the spiritual heart of Britain. In the stalwart Avalonians I don't see impractical space-cases. I see impeccable moral integrity and courage. Immense forces were surely at work. Dion Fortune gave her all during the war. She died shortly afterwards, exhausted on all levels by the intensity of her efforts. The rebirth of Glastonbury had begun at the start of the century with Bligh Bond's work at the Abbey. The magical Battle of Britain effectively completed that process.

FROM OUT OF THE MISTS

In recent times the return of the divine feminine has found increasing expression in Glastonbury. The life and work of Dion Fortune was an important precursor of the current era of the Goddess Conference. The Arthurian mythos likewise looms large. Some might speculate that what occultists would term the inner plane dynamic behind what manifested in the Arthurian Glastonbury resurgence in the sixties likewise owes a major debt to Dion Fortune's work.

The two elements most obviously came together in Marion Zimmer Bradley's *The Mists of Avalon*. She took on the not inconsiderable task of retelling the enormous Arthurian corpus with the female mysteries revitalised within it. In Celtic mythology the land was personified as a goddess who changed with the seasons. If the land was to thrive she had to be respected. Any king or hero had to be in right relationship with her. Beyond Morgan and Vivienne, Arthurian literature is full of female characters. Increasing attention has been given to them. There is a case to be made for seeing them as watered down remnants of figures that had either been goddesses or priestesses of their cults, the most obvious being Guenevere herself. The Round Table, representing the land, was part of the bridal dowry in certain respects.

The Mists of Avalon was another major moment in the development of the rebirth of the literature of the Matter of Britain. Dion Fortune had been a big influence. Her idea that Arthur, Merlin, and Morgan were titles that were handed down through the ages was featured throughout. In this version Morgan is very much the heroine. If the story has a failing it may be that Guenevere is not portrayed sympathetically. Literary snobs hate the book. Pagan snobs hate it. Dark Age history nerds hate it. They may all be missing the point. There have been numerous people moved to the very core of their being by it. Some have crossed oceans to come to Glastonbury as a result. Its modern mythos hangs heavy in the Somerset air. In 1999 Marion Zimmer Bradley's ashes were scattered from the Tor, her spirit assuredly being welcomed into the Avalon of the Heart.

A Note on Melchizedec

MELCHIZEDEC IS ONE OF THE MOST enigmatic characters in the Bible and therefore an esoteric favourite. He has a walk-on part in chapter 14 of *Genesis* when he meets Abraham after the latter has achieved victory in a battle. *"Melchizidec king of Salem brought forth bread and wine: and he was priest of God Most High. And he blessed him, and said, Blessed be Abraham of God Most high, possessor of heaven and earth".* So, he is a priest and a king and he has the authority to dispense blessings to the father of the Jewish race before the time of Moses. In Christian times he came to be regarded as some kind of mysterious prefiguration of Christ for his proto-eucharistic feast, getting another brief mention in the *Epistle to the Hebrews* on that basis.

Rene Guenon stated that 'Melki-Tsedeq' was acting on behalf of the spiritual hierarchy of the planet and embodies the Lord of the World spoken of in connection with Agharthi and Shambhala. The meeting with Abraham was, *"a spiritual investiture, wherein is found the exact point of union between the Hebraic and the great primordial tradition."* Melchizedek appears in some Byzantine artwork and later is depicted by statues in some of the Gothic cathedrals such as Chartres, Notre Dame and Reims. As the bearer of a chalice it's not surprising that he has been linked with the Grail and the possibility of some hidden sect.

St Paul mentions the little matter that Melchizedek, *"is without father, without mother, without origin — has neither beginning nor end to his life"* and, *"dwells as Priest in perpetuity."* This seems to suggest immortality. It's on that basis that he now functions as what the New Agers call an Ascended Master.

Dion Fortune believed that Melchizedec was the inner plane chief of her magical order, which featured three 'rays' of emanation. Each ray also had a subsidiary Master in charge of it. The Green Ray was an Earth Mysteries path. It involved connection to the faery realm. These ideas had crystalised for Dion Fortune during time spent at Glastonbury. She had contacted Melchizedec on the Tor and he had shown her the three rays and their Lords.

The occultists of Dion Fortune's epoch thought of Melchizedek and the Archangel Michael as two separate beings. Today's New Agers have taken that on. Some of the Dead Sea Scrolls literature discovered in 1947 makes it clear that there were apocalypse obsessed Jews who believed they were one and the same. Guenon mentions that *"Taking the strict sense of the name 'Melki-Tsedeq', as 'King of Justice', his proper attributes are the same scales and sword that characterize Mikael, 'Angel of Judgement'"*.

A Glastonbury Qabalah

A T THE TIME OF THE FIFTIETH ANNIVERSARY of the end of the Second
World War in 1995, I was inspired to recreate Dion Fortune's visualisation of the inner realm of the Tor. The result was entirely satisfying and I gave
considerable attention to it during the time of my moving to Glastonbury
shortly after. On December 6th 1996, in acknowledgement of her birthday, I
put on a public event in Glastonbury with the intention of using the same
material again to see how a group of people would respond to it in the modern world. I was very aware, through reading the wartime letters collected
together and published by Gareth Knight as *The Magical Battle of Britain*,
that Fortune believed the Glastonbury work was not just relevant to the
immediate circumstance of the war but also to the regeneration of the national consciousness in the future and the birth of a New Age.

As the time drew near I found that I spontaneously thought of vivid
imagery that developed from the original core to create a full Glastonbury
Qabalah. Notice that I term it *a* Glastonbury Qabalah, not *the* Glastonbury
Qabalah. I claim no exclusivity or definitiveness about it. It may mutate as
time dictates. The main point is that cultivating a feeling for 'British music'
and the Grail epoch material so important to the western mystery tradition
was a vital precondition for the appearance of such inspiration. Much work
was later done with this revival and expansion of Dion Fortune's work,
including an episode on the night of Princess Diana's funeral, but that forms
part of another tale.

This material is presented in a form which can be used for pathworking
visualisations if desired.

The Company of the Avalon of the Heart invite you to join them.

Come, by whatever means, to the cavern in the Mount of Illumination,
where the brethren assemble and those who come in light appear. In the air
hangs, in a blaze of light, a red rose on a cross of gold or, for those with such
a background, the Golden Dawn Rose Cross in all its complex detail. This
image is of the sphere of Tiphareth, realm of the sun, equilibrium and

harmony. By its light is the cavern made visible. A celestial perpetual choir intones unseen in the background.

Be aware that a winding stone staircase cut in the rock joins the cavern with other chambers above and below it.

Beneath is a path that reaches deep into the earth where dwell ancient ones, ancestors, faery folk, elementals, chthonic deities.

Immediately above the cavern is a Hall of Learning, a library, where volumes of arcane knowledge await the seeker. Look in its books for answers to your deepest questions.

Above this is a Grail Chapel. A place of devotion and grace, of sublime spiritual power. This corresponds to the physical space of the church and monastery atop the Tor.

The Tor tower is the physical sign of an inner plane Watchtower where a silent watcher, cowled and cloaked, stands in perpetual vigil, seeing the inner tides of the destiny of nations.

All of these places are accessible but let those who would join the Watcher's vigil take heed of the warning that here is a place of power not suitable for all.

Having sensed the other chambers of the Hill of Vision focus again on the cavern lit by the Rose Cross.

Above the cross, from the realm of Kether, the most high, a sphere of white light appears. Within it as vision and presence emerges the figure of Christ. He wears a diamond encrusted crown of pure white brilliance flecked with gold.

Beneath the cross appears a purple sphere of light. Yesod. Within it a vision of Glastonbury Abbey on a full moon night. The Virgin Mary walks along the centre of its ruins. She wears a black cloak covered with shining silver stars. A crescent moon adorns her head. She carries a Grail Chalice. The geometric grid plan of the Abbey foundations light up in silver from beneath the ground. The presence of the monks of the Company of Avalon can be sensed all around.

To the right of the centre of the cross a blue sphere. Chesed. Within it, seated on a stone crystal throne, is Merlin. He is dressed in blue-violet and deep purple and is holding a diamond sceptre and orb. Representing the most archaic of lineages, he wears a stag-antlered headpiece. A unicorn can be glimpsed somewhere behind him.

Opposite, to the left of the centre of the cross, a red sphere forms in the air. Geburah. Here is Arthur, sitting on a stationary white horse, holding aloft the sword Excalibur.

So is a cross formulated that harmonises Glastonbury and Britain's Christian and Pagan heritage. Around the four points of the Rose Cross the images hover in their spheres of coloured light in the great cavern. Four more spheres will now join them.

On the right above Merlin's sphere, but a little below the level of that of Christ, a grey ball of light appears. Chokmah. In it a vision of Wearyall hill. It is daylight. A grey mist surrounds the foot of the hill like a sea. The sky above is a clear spring blue. Across it can be seen shining the outline forms of the Glastonbury Zodiac. The Holy Thorn comes into focus. It is in bloom. Joseph of Arimathea is standing with his right outstretched hand around its trunk. He is facing to the left towards the Tor so we see in profile his bearded face.

Opposite, above the sphere of Arthur, comes Binah. Firstly a black sphere like ink. In that deep dense liquid darkness many flickering points of light can be seen. Moving nearer to them in vision they reveal themselves as innumerable candles. The location is the Chalice Well gardens at night. Many are present for a rite of silent contemplation. In the inner sanctum around the well-head, the vesica piscis cover is raised and its metalwork shines with reflected candle light. Standing to its left and facing right, wearing a black outer robe of concealment, is Morgan. A raven is perched on her shoulder. In the shadows behind, sensed more than seen, is another presence. A mature woman. Dion Fortune herself.

Beneath Merlin and the cross but above the level of Mary, on the right forms a green sphere. Netzah. In here is Chalice Hill in spring sunshine. The Tor can be seen behind. All around are spring flowers. Bees hover and buzz about them. Now comes a naked Venus like Botticelli's. She wears a head-dress of roses. Women looking like the graces of *Primavera* accompany her.

They are the Melissae, the Bee Priestesses. This is the inner plane realm of their secret garden. They are keeping bees for an alchemical nectar. Somewhere beyond the Tor they work their rites of the Chalice of Green Fire to bring a vision of beauty triumphant to earth.

Opposite, beneath Arthur, an orange sphere. Hod. Bride's Mound as it is physically today. Superimposed upon the scene its inner plane reality as sanctuary and powerhouse of Brigit. A perpetual flame is burning. Priestesses go about their duties. Brigit stands to the forefront holding a snake staff.

Within the cavern now is access to a complete Glastonbury Qabalah and the chambers of the cavern itself. Any of these realms can be worked within. Perhaps connections seek to be made between them. And the conduit of manifestation, the earthing in Malkuth, is we ourselves and our lives that change through connection with these ideas. And it is the land itself. Following the end of an epochal century of word-historical destiny, Great Britain needs to take stock of its sacred history and inner resources to regenerate itself for the vast unknown future.

Let there be no misconception that because Christ, Mary, Merlin and Arthur represent old traditions that they are now ineffectual, outmoded and generally redundant. These forces were, at one point in the war, bravely invoked by Dion Fortune to purge the nation of all that was corrupt and inert so that progress could be made. This can be done again. Masks that these beings are given by different eras can likewise be purged and their raw essence remains. Arthur and Merlin are no staid Victorian gentlemen when they are contacted today. Indeed, during the two minutes silence on VE Day 1995, before the lighting of beacon fires across the nation, Arthur Pendragon was seen by one person as naked and powerfully ithyphallic within the Tor. The mysteries of Sophia and the Magdalene are now explicitly inherent in the Abbey vision of Mary. And an ever more enigmatic and powerful Gnostic, Essene, Buddhist, Druid, Magician, revolutionary (the list is endless) Christ calls the many emanations of the One to unity at the divine heart that is Consciousness itself. Is it any wonder that the totality of the mystery that Glastonbury represents is activating ever more strongly and that a beacon shines from the Mount of Illumination? Light your own torch from it and go forth. Now is the time.

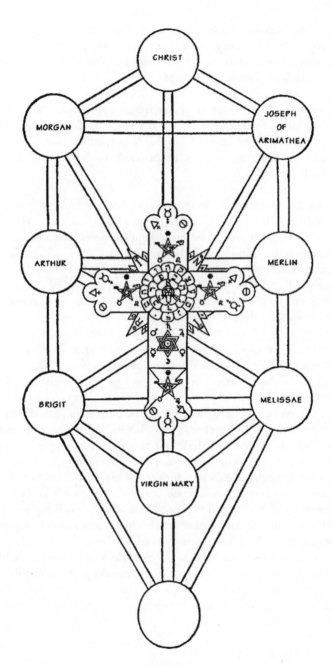

A GLASTONBURY QABALAH

Bibliography

Ackroyd, Peter, *Albion*, Chatto & Windus, London, 2002.

Anderson, Flavia, *The Ancient Secret*, Thorsons, Wellingborough, 1987.

Ashe, Geoffrey, *King Arthur's Avalon*, London, 1957.

Ashe, Geoffrey, *Camelot and the Vision of Albion*, William Heinemann, UK, 1971.

Ashe, Geoffrey, *The Ancient Wisdom*, Macmillan, London, 1977.

Ashe, Geoffrey, *Avalonian Quest*, Methuen, London, 1982.

Ashe, Geoffrey, *Kings and Queens of Early Britain*, Methuen, London, 1982.

Ashe, Geoffrey, *The Finger and the Moon*, William Heinemann Ltd, 1973.

Baigent, Michael, & Leigh, Richard, & Lincoln, Henry, *The Holy Blood and the Holy Grail*, Corgi, 1983.

Baigent, Michael & Leigh, Richard, *The Elixir and the Stone*, Viking, England, 1997.

Baillie, Mike, *Exodus to Arthur*, Batsford, London, 1999.

Barber, Richard, *The Figure of Arthur*, Longman Group Ltd, London, 1972.

Barber, Richard, *King Arthur in Legend and History*, Cardinal, London, 1973.

Barber, Richard, *The Devil's Crown*, BBC, London, 1978.

Barber, Richard, *The Holy Grail*, Allen Lane, London, 2004.

Benham, Patrick, *The Avalonians*, Gothic Image, Glastonbury, 1993.

Biddle, Martin, *King Arthur's Round Table*, Boydell Press, UK, 2000.

Blyton, Enid, *Tales of Brave Adventure*, Deans International Publishing, London, 1963.

Bobko, Jane, ed, with Newman, Barbara, and Fox, Matthew, *Vision: the Life and Music of Hildegard Von Bingen*, Viking Penguin, USA, 1995.

Boorman John, *Adventures of a Suburban Boy*, Faber & Faber, London, 2003.

Bradley, Marion Zimmer, *The Mists of Avalon*, Del Rey books, USA, 1987.

Broadhurst, Paul, *Tintagel and the Arthurian Mythos*, Pendragon Press, Cornwall, 1992.

Brown, Rosemary Alicia, *Katharine Emma Maltwood Artist 1878-1961,* Sono Nis Press, Victoria BC, Canada, 1981.

Bryant, Nigel, Translator, *The High Book of the Grail,* DS Brewer, Cambridge, 1996.

Caine, Mary, *The Glastonbury Zodiac,* Surrey, 1978.

Caine, Mary, *Celtic Saints and the Glastonbury Zodiac,* Capall Bann, Berks, 1998.

Carley, James P, *Melkin the Bard and Esoteric Tradition at Glastonbury Abbey,* Downside Review, Vol 99, Bath, 1981.

Carley, James P, *Glastonbury Abbey,* Gothic Image Publications, Somerset, 1996.

Cavendish, Richard, *King Arthur and the Grail,* Granada Publishing, St Albans, 1980.

Chambers, EK, *Arthur of Britain,* Sidgwick & Jackson, London, 1927.

Cohn, Norman, *The Pursuit of the Millennium,* Oxford University Press, 1970.

Collins, Andrew, *Twenty-First Century Grail,* Virgin, London, 2004.

Cooper-Oakley, Isabel, *Masonry and Medieval Mysticism,* Theosophical Publishing House Ltd, London, 1900.

Darrah, John, *The Real Camelot,* Thames and Hudson, London, 1981.

Devereux, Paul, *Haunted Land,* Piatkus Books, London, 2001.

Duxbury, Brenda, & Williams, Michael, with Wilson, Colin, *King Arthur Country in Cornwall,* Bossiney Books, Cornwall, 1979.

Evans, Sebastian, Translator, *The High History of the Holy Grail,* James Clarke & Co Ltd, Cambridge.

Evola, Julius, *The Mystery of the Grail,* Inner Traditions International, 1997.

Fortune, Dion, *Avalon of the Heart,* London, 1934.

Fortune Dion, *The Mystical Qabalah,* London, 1935.

Fox, Matthew, *Original Blessing,* Bear & Co, Santa Fe, 1983.

Fulcanelli, *Le Mystere Des Cathedrals,* Neville Spearman Ltd, London, 1971.

Gale, Jack, *The Circle and the Square,* Capall Bann, Berkshire, 1997.

Geoffrey of Monmouth, *The History of the Kings of Britain,* Penguin Books, London, 1966.

Godwin, Joscelyn, *Arktos,* Thames and Hudson, London, 1993.

Goodrich, Norma Lorre, *The Holy Grail,* Harper Collins Publishers, New York, 1992.

Grigsby, John, *Warriors of the Wasteland*, Watkins, London, 2003.

Guenon, Rene, *The Lord of the World*, Coombe Springs Press, North Yorkshire, 1983.

Harrison, Hank, *The Cauldron and the Grail*, The Archives Press, California, 1992.

Hartley, Christine, *The Western Mystery Tradition*, London, 1967.

Heer, Friedrich, *The Medieval World*, George Weidenfeld & Nicholson Ltd, London, 1961.

Kahanne, Henry, & Kahanne Renee, *The Krater and the Grail: Hermetic Sources of the Parzival*, University of Illinois Press, USA, 1965.

Keys, David, *Catastrophe*, Arrow Books, London, 2000.

Kipling, Rudyard, *Pucks of Pook's Hill*, Macmillan & Co, London, 1926.

Knight, Christopher and Lomas, Robert, *The Hiram Key*, Century Books Ltd, UK, 1996.

Knight, Christopher and Lomas, Robert, *The Second Messiah*, Century Books Ltd, UK, 1997.

Knight, Gareth, *The Secret Tradition in Arthurian Legend*, Aquarian Press, Wellingborough, 1983.

Knight, Gareth, *The Magical Battle of Britain*, SIL, England, 1993.

Knight, Gareth, *Dion Fortune & the Inner Light*, Thoth Publications, Loughborough, 2000.

Leitch, Yuri, *Gwyn: Ancient god of Glastonbury and key to the Glastonbury Zodiac*, The Temple Publications, Somerset, 2007.

Loomis, Roger Sherman, *The Grail. From Celtic Myth to Christian Symbol*, Columbia University Press, USA, 1963.

Maltwood, Katharine, E. *A Guide to Glastonbury's Temple of the Stars*, James Clarke & Co, Cambridge, 1934.

Maltwood, Katharine, E. *The Enchantments of Britain*, James Clarke & Co, Cambridge, 1944.

Mann, Nicholas, R, *The Isle of Avalon*, Llewellyn, USA, 1996.

Markale, Jean, *King of the Celts*, Inner Traditions, Vermont, 1994.

Markale, Jean, *The Grail*, Inner Traditions, Vermont, 1999.

Matthews, John, *The Grail*, Thames and Hudson, London, 1981.

Matthews, John, *At the Table of the Grail*, Routledge & Kegan Paul, London, 1984.

Matthews, John, Ed, *The Household of the Grail,* Aquarian Press, Northamptonshire, 1990.

Matthews, John, Ed, *A Glastonbury Reader,* Aquarian Press, London, 1991.

Mellers, Wilfrid, *Vaughan Williams and the Vision of Albion,* Barrie and Jenkins Ltd, London, 1989.

Merry, Eleanor, *The Flaming Door,* Rider & Co, London, 1936.

Michell, John, *City of Revelation,* Abacus, UK, 1972.

Michell, John, *New Light on the Ancient Mystery of Glastonbury,* Gothic Image Publications, Glastonbury, 1990.

Miller, Hamish, & Broadhurst, Paul, *The Sun and the Serpent,* Pendragon Press, Cornwall, 1989.

Morton, HV, *In Search of England,* Methuen, London, 1927.

Nitze, William A & collaborators, *Perlesvaus, Volume 2,* Phaeton Press, New York, 1972.

Olschki, Leonardo, *The Grail Castle and its Mysteries,* Manchester University Press, UK, 1966.

Phillips, Graham, & Keatman Martin, *King Arthur: The True Story,* Century Random house, London, 1992.

Phillips, Graham, *The Chalice of the Magdalene,* Bear and Co, USA, 2004.

Powys, John Cowper, *A Glastonbury Romance,* Picador, London, 1975.

Rahn, Otto, *Crusade Against the Grail,* Inner Traditions, Vermont, 2006.

Rahtz, Philip, & Watts, Lorna, *Glastonbury. Myth and Archaeology.* Tempus Publishing Ltd, Gloucestershire. 2003.

Richardson, Alan, *Priestess,* Thoth Publications, Loughborough, 2007.

Scott, Ernest, *The People of the Secret,* Octagon Press Ltd, London, 1983.

Seddon, Richard, *The Mystery of Arthur at Tintagel,* Rudolf Steiner Press, London, 1990.

Sinclair, Andrew, *The Discovery of the Grail,* Century, London, 1998.

Smithett Lewis, Lionel, *Glastonbury 'The Mother of Saints' Her Saints,* AR Mowbray & Co Ltd, London, 1925.

Spence, Lewis, *The Mysteries of Britain,* Senate, Middlesex, 1994.

Stein, Walter Johannes, *The Ninth Century,* Temple Lodge Press, London, 1991.

Stein, Walter Johannes, *The Death of Merlin,* Floris Books, Edinburgh, 1989.

Steiner, Rudolf, *The Holy Grail,* Sophia Books, East Sussex, 2001.

Stewart,RJ, *The Complete Merlin Tarot,* Element, UK. 1992.

Stewart, RJ, *Merlin: The Prophetic Vision and the Mystic Life,* Arkana, UK, 1994.

Strachan, Gordon, *Chartres,* Floris Books, Edinburgh, 2003.

Strong, Roy, *The Spirit of Britain,* Pimlico, London, 2000.

Tennyson, Alfred, The Works of Alfred Lord Tennyson, Macmillan & Co, London, 1889.

Weidner, Jay, & Bridges, Vincent, *The Mysteries of the Great Cross at Hendaye,* Destiny Books, Vermont, 2003.

Weston, Jessie, *The Quest of the Holy Grail,* G Bell & Sons Ltd, London, 1913.

Weston, Jessie, *From Ritual to Romance,* Princeton University Press, West Sussex, 1993.

Wilson Knight, G, *The Saturnian Quest,* Methuen & Co Ltd, London, 1964.

Wood, Michael, *In Search of England,* Penguin Books, London, 2000.

Woodcock, Peter, *This Enchanted Isle,* Gothic Image, Glastonbury, 2000.

HANK HARRISON

I have read a number of online articles by Harrison, primarily on *Perlesvaus.* They included *Signs of Divinity, Eleanore's Ghost, The Mystery, Gawain's Quest, Who Wrote Y Saent Graal?, Who Was Ina?*

These items can be hard to find and seem to periodically disappear from view. They often seem to be in the form of first drafts and full of typos and errors. Checking the availability of a number of them at the time of completing this work I could find virtually nothing at the original addresses. What does remain is *The Grail in the Stones.* Google it. This contains the material on Gildas and Chartres, including a photo of the mural that may well have considerable significance. I have never been able to get this picture to display over 3 years and 3 different computers! It took me a lot of effort to find Harrison's material and read it. Even though I may not entirely endorse it I consider the effort to have been entirely worthwhile. It would be great to see his stuff tidied up and brought together in print one day. The man deserves recognition.